MICROBIUM

Fig. 1. Detail from Hieronymus Bosch, *Ship of Fools* (1490–1500)

First published in 2023 by punctum books, Earth, Milky Way.
https://punctumbooks.com

ISBN-13: 978-1-68571-170-2 (print)
ISBN-13: 978-1-68571-171-9 (ePDF)

DOI: 10.53288/396.1.00

LCCN: 2023943269
Library of Congress Cataloging Data is available from the Library of Congress

Book design: Hatim Eujayl and Vincent W.J. van Gerven Oei
Cover image: Detail from "Monster soup commonly called Thames water."
Coloured etching by W. Heath, 1828. Wellcome Collection.

p. punctumbooks

spontaneous acts of scholarly combustion

HIC SVNT MONSTRA

microbium
the neglected lives
of micro-matter

edited by
joela jacobs &
agnes malinowska

p.

Contents

Acknowledgments

This book wouldn't have been possible without the ideas generated in a seminar of the American Comparative Literature Association in 2018. There, we were fortunate to meet and develop our thinking around micro-matter with a variety of kind and brilliant people, some of whom have contributed to the present volume. We are likewise grateful to the Association for the Study of Literature and Environment for giving us a forum to continue thinking together about micro-matter at their annual conference in 2019 and then again in 2021. Our authors have been a pleasure to work with, and we thank them for their creativity, insight, and patience in molding their writing to fit the goals of this unusual micro-book. As the idea for the book was initially coming together, we realized that it would be a difficult format to place for publication, which is one of many reasons why we are indebted to the team at punctum books for sharing our vision and taking on this project. The principles of the press are close to our hearts and working together has been a joy; we are so grateful for the effort and care that punctum has poured into this little book. None of us could have known how much the world of micro-matter would come to matter a year after our first seminar, and we thank our authors and publisher for tackling the challenges that came with the COVID-19 pandemic with such grace. We, the editors, also thank each other for a collaboration that felt like a true partnership and an opportunity for mutual learning and growth. Last but not least, we are grateful to all the forms of matter, whether macro- or micro-, that sustain our lives and support us in our work and play.

Introduction

Joela Jacobs and Agnes Malinowska

In 2020, the invisible realm of micro-matter came to shape our lives in unprecedented ways. A virus so small that it is only visible through advanced electron microscopes suddenly threatened global economies, brought healthcare systems to the brink of collapse, pushed countless people into extreme poverty, amplified fierce political and social divisions, and most devastatingly, caused the deaths of millions of people worldwide. SARS-CoV-2 overturned the ordinary ways we work, care, learn, play, and sustain ourselves. It threw massive global inequalities into relief, while fueling emergent ones. As we write this introduction three years into the pandemic, it is clear that COVID-19 is only the most recent and glaring example of how profoundly the patterns of activity and exchange in the invisible realm of micro-matter reverberate onto the scale of human life. This book tells the story of such tiny causes of upheaval and illuminates the foundational role they play in the ongoing story of life on earth. Micro-matter such as viruses can throw lives and systems into complete disarray. But no life could survive without the invisible community of microorganisms that silently props up our human and more-than-human social networks.

We call this book *Microbium* to mark its place in the tradition of the herbarium, which collects various plant specimens and can serve as a record of scientific, cultural, and historical knowledge. At the same time, the name *Microbium* is an affectionate tribute to the idea of the microbiome, the diverse communities of microorganisms that inhabit and sustain a given environment. The human microbiome is a wild interspecies assemblage of countless microbial species, and humans survive and flourish only to the extent that this micro-community does. Our *Microbium* zooms in on eight types of micro-matter whose outsized significance can be easy for humans to forget or neglect. In addition to viruses, there are animalcules, bacteria, corals, fungi, lichen, pollen, and protozoa. Each entry describes the natural history and scientific discovery of its particular micro-matter, while also telling a story about the cultural significance it has taken on over the centuries.

The authors of the *Microbium* are a collection of scholars and artists working in a variety of disciplines, genres, and institutional contexts across North America and Europe. We asked each of them to consider three questions related to how their chosen micro-matters fit in our world. First, how does this form of matter live in the micro-scale? In response, each author drew on current research in the biological sciences to explain the basic makeup and vital functions of their micro-matter in its natural habitats and in relation to the macro-scale of human life. The world as humans know it has always teemed with micro-matter, and microbes form the evolutionary basis of all life on earth. At the same time, the development of the modern microscope in the seventeenth century revolutionized the way that people saw the world by making this invisible realm newly available to human perception. Suddenly, each drop of water was revealed to be a cosmopolitan society of diverse "animalcules," as microorganisms were once called by early microscopists. This previously unknown layer of the world fundamentally transformed the natural sciences and helped change the way that humans saw themselves. As scientists puzzled over the place of humans in earth's story, they now also had the microbial order to consider as a possible antecedent to the human. A central term in this book, "protozoa," was, for instance, introduced to describe the first unicellular organisms on earth, the very origins of *all* life. And yet the drive to rank and order micro-matter in its baffling complexity itself produced messiness and instability. Once a potent category, protozoa soon became a confusing taxonomical dumping ground for a variety of rather dissimilar organisms.

The second question that we asked our authors to consider bears on how and why micro-matter has been either neglected or attended to. Here, they turned to the cultural history of their micro-matter, paying special attention to how this history has inflected or been inflected by the most pressing social debates of a given time and place. An emblematic example discussed in this book is the case of Mary Mallon or "Typhoid Mary," the Irish American cook famously demonized in the early years of the twentieth century for being the first known asymptomatic carrier of any disease. Sentenced to life in quarantine by public health officials, Mary held together some of the period's most vexing tensions around race, gender, and class in her silently contagious body. Perhaps lesser known is the moral panic spurred by the discovery that pollen is plant sperm, which rendered eighteenth-century women's engagement with flowers and botany suddenly scandalous.

Third, we asked our authors to theorize why their micro-matter matters and to whom. Our entries reveal the microscopic dimension to be a diverse network of multispecies collaborations and social experiments, as in, for instance, the composite organism lichen, which emerges from a symbiotic relationship between a fungus and algae or bacteria. Or take corals, which thrive as a partnership between animals and algae, while making home and kin across a dizzying array of species boundaries and national borders. These alliances point us to an image of life outside of individuality, life as essentially relational and generative, multiplying. If we follow the lead of bacteria, for instance, we end up with a politics of radical sociality that incites the individual to slip into the collective at every turn. Fungi likewise offer an alternative social order, one that would replace competition and hierarchy with kinship and interdependence. Taken as a whole, the entries in this book are marked by an eagerness to learn from micro-matter, to let it teach us how to revitalize our political and cultural systems, habits of thought, and aesthetic or representational modes.

While *Microbium* relies on the natural sciences and cultural history to tell the story of micro-matter, examples from the arts and literature lend texture to these miniscule lives, scaling them up, as it were, to dimensions better suited to human perception and feeling. With this in mind, we conceive of each entry as a "microscopic reading": a mini-reading of visual or literary artworks. From the poetry of Emily Dickinson to contemporary stories about the COVID-19 pandemic, our collective analysis stresses the role of art as a kind of cultural microscope in its own right — an instrument for observing the invisible interspecies social realm and translating its significance to the scale of human culture.

Welcome to our *Microbium*! We hope you enjoy this journey to the invisible foundations of life on earth.

CHAPTER 1

Animalcules

Ada Smailbegović

> In the world of the imagination, it becomes normal for an
> elephant, which is an enormous animal, to come out of a snail
> shell. It would be exceptional, however, if we were to ask him to
> go back into it.
> — Gaston Bachelard, *The Poetics of Space*

It is perhaps unusual to begin an entry on micro-animals with
an invocation of a large animal, an animal as large as an elephant. In the chapter, "Shells," in *The Poetics of Space,* the French
philosopher Gaston Bachelard posits an imaginative paradox
of proportion by creating an image of an enormous elephant
emerging out of a tiny snail shell. This unfolding of a large
body out of a disproportionately small space appears possible
as a thought experiment until we imagine its reversal—the elephant somehow folding itself back up, until it assumes the size
of the snail again. Strangely, the figure of the elephant appears
also in the writings of one of the early microscopists, the Dutch
scientist Antonie van Leeuwenhoek, who was the first human
observer to take note of micro-animals. Leeuwenhoek pointed
out that even though such minute animals dwell in the intimate
spaces of our houses they are "by reason of [...] [their] minute-

ness, unknown to or unobserved by many" (Leeuwenhoek 1800, 173). In his work, "Of the Mite," Leeuwenhoek refutes the theory of spontaneous generation, circulating in the seventeenth and eighteenth centuries, and argues that it is as "impossible for an elephant to be brought forth from dust or dirt" as it is "for a Mite to be bred out of meal or any corrupted substance" (173). In using the example of a large animal, such as an elephant, Leeuwenhoek vividly illustrates for the reader how unlikely it would be for any living being, even a tiny mite, to simply arise fully formed from a heap of inanimate matter.

In these observations, Leeuwenhoek addresses not only the scale of the mite, its minuteness, but also the limitations of human perception, which render it nearly invisible to the human sensorium. In this context, Leeuwenhoek's invocation of an elephant begins to act as a figurative microscope, a frame of reference allowing the mite to grow in proportion until it can occupy a clearer space in the human sensory world. While observing the mite through the lens of an actual microscope, Leeuwenhoek resorts to his metaphoric microscope once again to describe the hairs that cover the head of the mite: "When a Mite touched these hairs, while cleaning its head, in the manner that cats and other animals do, the hairs when moved out of their place recovered themselves with a kind of spring, whereupon I thought that these hairs might be designed to protect the eyes" (172–73). In this case, the mite appears cat-like, and the human observer projects the image of the larger animal ubiquitously grooming itself onto the mite's tiny scale and unfamiliar shape. One could argue that a parallel process of metaphoric amplification is also at work when micro-animals such as tardigrades are described by contemporary scientists as "water bears." This term, in fact, can also be traced to an earlier moment of scientific observation and the work of the German zoologist Johann August Ephraim Goeze, who in 1773 observed these tiny animals for the first time and named them *kleiner Wasserbär* or "little water bears" on account of the manner of their movement, which resembles the gait of a bear.

I bring up these examples not only because I am struck by the beauty of metaphor in its capacity to amplify perception, but also because they point to the relative limits of how the human sensorium perceives scale. It is in this way that such examples get to the heart of the very definition of what a small animal is. They implore us to ask: small in relation to *what? Small* according to *whose* capacities for perception? Such questions attempt to acknowledge how anthropocentric the concept of scale can be and how the very definition of smallness is, at its heart, relative and relational. In order to proceed in a less anthropocentric way, one might ask how different perceptual systems navigate the question of scale. In thinking about small animals not just as objects of scientific and even aesthetic fascination, but also as subjects with their own capacities for perception, the materiality of the world opens onto microscopic topographies with features relevant to the micro-animals that inhabit them, even if they are imperceptible to the human sensorium. In other words, what may appear as an insignificant droplet of matter to a human observer may open up, within the perceptual increments of another organism's sensorium, into a whole microcosm or an entire topography that makes up a world.

Varieties of Animalcules and Their Movements

Under the lens of Leeuwenhoek's microscope, different material samples were transformed into the intricate topographies of microscopic worlds, with a variety of small creatures moving across them. Leeuwenhoek named these microscopic organisms "animalcules," from the Latin *animalculum* or "tiny animal." This archaic term included a broader range of microscopic organisms than the contemporary term micro-animal, among them single-celled protozoa and even bacteria. While microanimals are very small, they are animals, and this makes them distinct from other tiny creatures. Unlike bacteria, they are eukaryotes, which means that their genetic material is enclosed in a nucleus. Moreover, they are multicellular, and, as most animals, are aerobic or oxygen-breathing, heterotrophic in that they ingest organic substances to sustain themselves, and motile during at least some parts of their lifecycle.

In his early observations of animalcules, Leeuwenhoek was struck by the sheer variety of their shapes and their diverse capacities for movement (see fig. 1). Some of these he describes as "roundish," some as "oval," noting that some of these last ones possessed "two leggs [sic] near the head, and two little fins on the other end of the body," and he also describes them as possessing "divers colours, some being whitish, others pellucid; others had green and very shining little scales" (Leeuwenhoek 1674, 182). As these forms pool both underneath the lens of his microscope and within the language of his prose, Leeuwenhoek turns his eye to the question of movement in particular, noting that the motion of most of these animalcules "in the water was so swift, and so various, upwards, downwards, and round about, that I confess I could not but wonder at it" (182). He describes some of these as being oval in shape "with certain short and slender organs or limbs, [...] by means of which they caused a kind of circular motion and current in the water" (207). On another occasion, he observes a different species, also in rainwater, which has an entirely distinct pattern of movement so that when the animalcules "would move from place to place, they brought their hind parts nearer to the fore part, and then, loosing the fore part, they extended it in like manner as we see caterpillars do" (Leeuwenhoek 1800, 208). Others moved as if by a motion of "small wheels set round the edges with sharp points or pins" (210). This particular, nearly mechanical-seeming pattern of motion leaves Leeuwenhoek with a sense of a "spectacle [...] wonderful and incomprehensible," as he cannot conceive "how such a motion can be produced or performed in an animal body" (210). These modes of motility may be recognizable to the modern reader as the hair-like extensions of cilia and flagella, which can propel single-celled organisms through the water, and the pseudopodia, which can extend, through a kind of streaming movement of the cytoplasm or the inner contents of the cell against the cell membrane, to produce a malleable and temporary limb. And, finally, the incomprehensible wheels that Leeuwenhoek observed belong to micro-animals known as "rotifers" or "wheel animalcules."

There is something wondrous about the figurative bestiary that seems to open up in many of Leeuwenhoek's descriptions in which the minute universe of animalcules is amplified through comparison with organisms and entities that are perceptible at scales accessible to the human senses. This seems particularly vivid when envisioning their movement, as in the moment when the inching along of a caterpillar is transposed onto the style of movement exhibited by one of the animalcules. But such modes of amplification also serve to subdivide even the minute world visible through the microscope into many different scales. Leeuwenhoek notes, for instance, that some of the animalcules that he locates in rainwater are "above a thousand times smaller than the smallest ones, which I have hitherto seen in cheese, wheaten flower, mould, and the like" (Leeuwenhoek 1674, 182). He goes on to compare these rainwater animalcules with cheese mites, concluding his assessment of their size with the following ratio: "I make the proportion of one of these small Water-creatures to a Cheese-mite, to be like that of a Bee to a Horse" (Leeuwenhoek 1676, 823). Some of these slightly larger, but still microscopic creatures, are perhaps closer to what we would today call micro-animals. Dust mites are, for instance, one such animal living on dust particles in most homes. Others, like tardigrades, have evolved to survive even in the most inhospitable environments, withstanding exposure to extreme temperatures, pressures, and even radiation. They have the capacity to shrink the surface area of their bodies to reduce dehydration by entering a dormant state that can last for more than a decade and have survived even in outer space. Most often, they are found covering the surfaces of mosses and lichen or in marine and freshwater sediments.

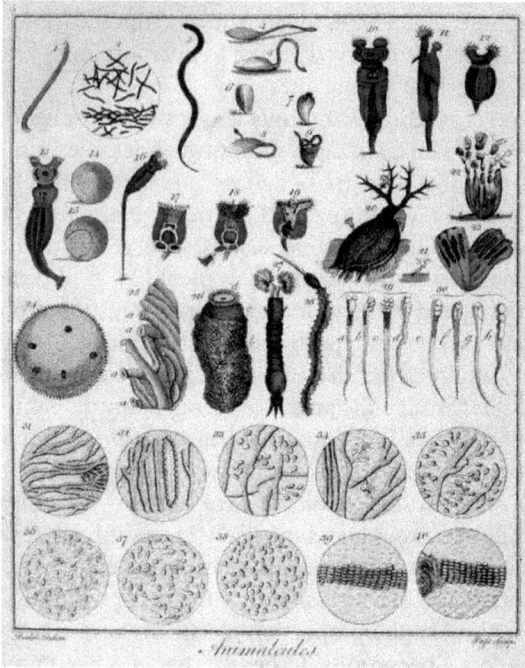

Fig. 1. An illustration of Antonie van Leeuwenhoek's animalcules, unknown artist, 1795.

Nested Topographies of the Microcosm

As micro-animals come to mix with and inhabit various kinds of animate and inanimate matter, they force us to reimagine the relationship between topography and scale. In this context, a grain of dust or the barbs of a waterfowl feather are transformed from minute material objects within the scales of the human world into vast landscapes, which constitute whole habitable worlds of their own. A sense that any speck of matter can open up into an entire tiny universe is evident in the work of the English scientist Robert Hooke, another famous early microscopist who described his microscopic observations in his book *Micrographia* from 1665. Hooke observes an entire universe under the

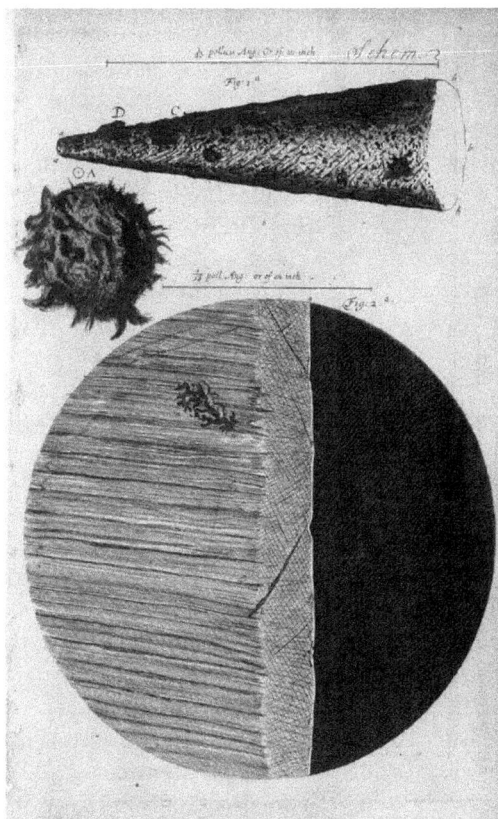

Fig. 2. Tip of a needle and a razor's edge, in Robert Hooke, *Micrographia,* 1665.

lens of his microscope, even as he is looking at what to a human observer appears as a simple speck of dirt: "The Earth it self, which lyes so neer us, under our feet, shews quite a new thing to us, and in every little particle of its matter; we now behold almost as great a variety of Creatures, as we were able before to reckon up in the whole Universe it self" (Hooke 1665, 18–19). In this sense, each particle of matter offers a complex topography inhabited by micro-animals. Hooke, for instance, observes a whole world populated by hundreds of mites living in the craters and crevices that exist at the point of a sharp needle (see fig. 2). Such an object, created through artifice, looks to the naked human eye to be smooth and finely formed, but, on a closer look, through a lens of the microscope, it reveals an unsettling realm of uneven surfaces, rugged chasms, and micro-abysses. These topographical features form a whole geography of "hills, and dales, and pores" that appears "big enough," Hooke suggests, "to have afforded a hundred armed Mites room enough to be rang'd by each other without endangering the breaking one anothers necks, by being thrust off on either side" (2). In this way a whole hypothetical world is revealed, consisting of a complex, uneven topography of abysses, chasms, and mountainous shapes on what to the unaided human eye or touch seems to be an uninterrupted slick, smooth surface.

Such an understanding of the microscopic dimensions of matter as containing complex miniature worlds inhabited by tiny animals revolutionized not only early science, but also came to shape the work of philosophers, who drew directly on the observations of the early microscopists in developing their metaphysical conceptualizations of reality. In 1676, the German philosopher Gottfried Wilhelm Leibniz, for instance, visited the Netherlands in order to meet Leeuwenhoek, writing in his correspondence subsequently that "'Mr. Leuwenhoek has shown' that there is 'an infinity of small animals in the least drop of water'" (quoted in Strickland 2014, 132). This allowed Leibniz to corroborate his sense that there were complex worlds to be found in even the smallest bit of matter, contributing empirical evidence for his cosmological view that different layers of material complexity are nested within one another to form infinitely recursive layers. In the *Monadology* from 1714, Leibniz writes about such an infinitely nested conception of materiality through the strikingly poetic image of a garden and a fishpond: "Each portion of matter may be conceived as a garden full of plants, and as a pond full of fish. But each branch of a plant, each limb of an animal, each drop of its humours, is also such a garden or such a pond" (Leibniz 2014, 28). In this scene, an infinite recursivity is at play, so that minute increments or droplets of matter that populate the initial pond are themselves sites of another such garden or pond and so on to infinity at increasingly tiny scales.

Tiny Animals = Tiny Perceptions

While many contemporary scientific articles on micro-animals report on their ability to survive extreme conditions and attempt to uncover the molecular mechanisms that are behind these feats of endurance, they do not typically pose questions about what it is like for a micro-animal, whose ways of sensing are so different than those of humans, to navigate the topographies of the microcosm. The remainder of this entry on micro-animals attempts to address this question by uncovering in certain moments in history of science and philosophy imaginative leaps that have attempted to open up different scales and perceptual dimensions of nonhuman worlds. In his considerations of living organisms, Leibniz, for instance, had the insight that more senses may exist among other animals in addition to those of sight, hearing, smell, taste, and touch possessed by humans. Modern scientists are now aware "that birds can perceive ultraviolet light, that bats navigate via echolocation, and that catfish and sharks have an 'electrical sense' often referred to as electroreception" (Strickland 2014, 79). Leibniz similarly intuited that our sensory limitations may mean that some or perhaps even "most of the features of objects may be concealed from us" (79). In fact, Leibniz argued that many perceptions occur below the threshold of human consciousness. Writing about Leibniz's aesthetics in *The Fold: Leibniz and the Baroque,* the French philosopher Gilles Deleuze (2006, 99) refers to these as "tiny perceptions."

In order to understand Leibniz's tiny perceptions, it may be useful to consider the sound of the sea. While the sound of the sea is composed of countless individual waves, these are too similar to one another for the sensorium to pick out the sound of one specific wave. As such, Leibniz is concerned with sensations that occur at the edges of what is perceptible and even with how the imperceptible shapes and inflects what is perceived. Or, as Deleuze writes in *The Fold,* for Leibniz "every conscious perception implies [...] [an] infinity of minute perceptions" (99). Such tiny perceptions constitute "as much the passage from one perception to another" as they make up the "components of each perception" (99). For a particular perception to arise as a conscious perception, a sense of differentiation must emerge among the microperceptions that surround it. When it comes to the example of the sound of the sea, two waves must be perceived as minutely distinct from one another in order to "become part of a relation that can allow the perception of a third, one that 'excels' over the others and comes to consciousness (implying that we are near the shoreline)" (101).

The concept of tiny perceptions links the question of perception to that of scale. In this way, it offers a way to theorize not only the process through which perceptions gather to form the familiar features that make up the anthropocentric scales of human worlds, but it also offers a way to scale perception down in order to ascertain how micro-animals may perceive the topography of their environments. The resolution of perception that is available to a particular sensorium, in other words, affects which features of a particular world will become distinct as discrete entities. If a perception is composed of units that are not individually discernible by a particular sensorium, the distinct edges between such units become blurred, leading to an inability to distinguish between the discrete objects that make up a particular phenomenon.

In order to examine the relevance of Leibniz's tiny perceptions for expanding the understanding of how micro-animals may navigate the topography of their worlds, it may be useful to turn here to the writings of the early twentieth-century German biologist Jakob von Uexküll, who was concerned with understanding animals not just as objects of scientific inquiry, but in also asking how the animals themselves perceived their environments. Uexküll observed that each organism is enfolded within a sheath of sensations that comprises its world or what Uexküll called the *Umwelt*. This world of sensations, composed of touch, smell, hearing, sight, and any other sensory inputs, enfolds the animal "like four envelopes of an increasingly sheer garment" (Uexküll 2010, 107). Uexküll's understanding of sensation is attentive to scale in a way that makes it particularly relevant for coming to understand how micro-animals may delineate the features that make up the topography of their microcosm. Consider, for instance, this scene in which Uexküll describes how an object, in this case a flower stem, is transformed almost entirely as it passes from the perceptual world of one organism into another:

> A flower stem that in our Umwelt is a support for the flower, becomes a pipe full of liquid for the meadow spittlebug (*Philaenus spumarius*) who sucks out the liquid to build its foamy nest. The same flower stem becomes an upward path for the ant, connecting its nest with its hunting ground in the flower. For the grazing cow the flower stem becomes part of a tasty morsel of food for her to chew in her big mouth. (108)

These refocalizations of perspective offer a kind of wondrous malleability to the features that make up the universe of each of these organisms. Entities are transformed in texture, shape, and size depending on the perceptual scale and needs of each animal, so that what had at one moment acted as a source of a liquid that can be transfigured into a foamy architecture of a nest becomes a structural element of the landscape itself, a kind of bridge that can support a body of an animal as it navigates a precipice within its environment.

According to Uexküll, understanding different scales of perception involves not only attending to the size of different elements that make up the universe of a particular organism, but also understanding the relevance that a particular entity possesses for each animal. This allows different features of a microcosm to be ordered by the significance and the attention that they require in an organism's life, with topographical features that have an immediate impact on life visible in full size, while other, much vaster ones may appear imperceptible. Uexküll illustrates this by describing how different celestial bodies appear within the smaller Umwelt horizon of a mosquito: "When mosquitoes dance in the sunset, they do not see our big human sun, setting six kilometers away, but small mosquito suns that set about half a meter away. The moon and stars are absent from the sky of the mosquito" (108). A strikingly similar, although perhaps less imaginatively and more violently executed image emerges when Leeuwenhoek examines the eye of a dragonfly, excising the cornea and using it as a kind of lens through which to view the world from a perspective of a dragonfly. After removing the "tunica cornea," Leeuwenhoek (1800, 342) places "a lighted candle at a small distance, so that the light of it must pass through" the excised part of the eye. He then reports on the appearance of the candle as seen through the cornea, in a sense using the dragonfly eye as a kind of perceptual mask allowing him to postulate what it may be like to perceive the candle as the dragonfly does: "I then saw through it the flame of the candle inverted, and not a single one, but some hundreds of flames appeared to me, and these so distinctly (though wonderfully minute) that I could discern the motion or trembling in each of them" (342). In this moment, Leeuwenhoek experiments with decentering human perception and trying out what it may be like to perceive the world as a dragonfly does, and yet there are still clear limitations to his attempt to view the world through a sensorium of another animal. When it comes to micro-animals, scale compounds this difficulty because the resolution of sensation into tiny perceptions occurs differently depending on the limitations of a particular sensory apparatus, and this, in turn, comes to constitute the edges of the topographical features that make up the world of a particular organism. In this way, small animals come to unsettle the anthropocentric sense of scale, illustrating that each animal, no matter its size, finds itself inside its own rich universe of perceptions, with its own topography and its own celestial orientations, whether from an anthropocentric sense of scale it appears as big as an elephant or as small as a mite.

References and Further Reading

Bachelard, Gaston. 1994. *The Poetics of Space.* Translated by Maria Jolas. Boston: Beacon Press.

Becchi, Alessandro. 2017. "Between Learned Science and Technical Knowledge: Leibniz, Leeuwenhoek, and the School for Microscopists." In *Tercentenary Essays on the Philosophy and Science of Leibniz,* edited by Lloyd Strickland, Erik Vynckier, and Julia Weckend, 47–80. Cham: Palgrave Macmillan.

Deleuze, Gilles. 2006. *The Fold: Leibniz and the Baroque.* Translated by Tom Conley. London: Continuum.

Erdmann, Weronika, and Łukasz Kazmarek. 2017. "Tardigrades in Space Research: Past and Future." *Origins of Life and Evolution of Biospheres* 47, no. 4: 545–53. DOI: 10.1007/s11084-016-9522-1.

Hooke, Robert. 1665. *Micrographia: or Some Physiological Descriptions of Minute Bodies Made by Magnifying Glasses with Observations and Inquiries Thereupon.* London: Jo. Martyn and Ja. Allestry. https://digital.sciencehistory.org/works/9g54xj51s.

Lane, Nick. 2015. "The Unseen World: Reflections on Leeuwenhoek (1677) 'Concerning Little Animals.'" *Philosophical Transactions of the Royal Society B: Biological Sciences* 370, no. 1666: 1–10. DOI: 10.1098/rstb.2014.0344.

van Leeuwenhoek, Antonie. 1674. "More Observations from Mr. Leewenhook, in a Letter of Sept. 7, 1674. Sent to the Publisher." *Philosophical Transactions of the Royal Society of London* 9, no. 108 (November 23): 178–82. DOI: 10.1098/rstl.1674.0057.

———. 1963. "Observations, Communicated to the Publisher by Mr. Antony van Leewenhoeck, in a Dutch Letter of the 9th Octob. 1676. Here English'd: Concerning Little Animals by Him Observed in Rain-Well-Sea- and Snow Water; As Also in Water wherein Pepper had Lain Infused." *Philosophical Transactions of the Royal Society of London* 12: 821–31. https://www.jstor.org/stable/101758.

————.. 1800. *The Select Works of Antony van Leeuwenhoek, Containing his Microscopical Discoveries in Many of the Works of Nature.* 2 vols. Translated by Samuel Hoole. London: G. Sidney, Black-Horse Court, Fleet-Street.

Leibniz, Gottfried Wilhelm. 2014. *Leibniz's "Monadology": A New Translation and Guide.* Translated by Lloyd Strickland. Edinburgh: Edinburgh University Press.

Møbjerg, Nadja, Kenneth Halberg, Aslak Jørgensen, Dennis Persson, M. Bjørn, Hans Ramløv, and Reinhardt Møbjerg Kristensen. 2011. "Survival in Extreme Environments: On the Current Knowledge of Adaptations in Tardigrades." *Acta Physiologica* 202, no. 3: 409–20. DOI: 10.1111/j.1748-1716.2011.02252.

Strickland, Lloyd. 2014. "The *Monadology:* Text with Running Commentary." In *Leibniz's "Monadology": A New Translation and Guide,* 39–161. Edinburgh: Edinburgh University Press.

von Uexküll, Jakob. 2010. *A Foray into the Worlds of Animals and Humans, with A Theory of Meaning.* Translated by Joseph D. O'Neil. Minneapolis: University of Minnesota Press.

CHAPTER 2

Bacteria

Agnes Malinowska

Bacteria may rightfully scoff at the idea that mere size renders them in some way diminutive or negligible. If they evade human perception, these microorganisms are arguably earth's darlings, its favorite children. They can survive in just about any ecosystem, no matter how hot or cold. In consequence, they flourish like no other life. The sheer number of bacteria far outstrips that of any other organism, and it has been estimated that, tiny as they are, bacteria's total biomass exceeds that of all other organisms combined. They are excellent earth citizens too. Among other feats, they break down dead matter, releasing nutrients for other life forms, and likewise convert atmospheric nitrogen and carbon into usable forms. Key to the survival of all life, bacteria also loom large in life's origins. Arriving some 1.5 billion years after earth was formed, bacteria were the planet's only living occupants for the next 3 billion years. A full three quarters of life's history belong to bacteria alone. The Cambrian explosion that gave rise to most plants and animals occurred a mere 540 million years ago.

Bacteria's central role in the story of life is reflected in biological taxonomy, which groups organisms into three domains. Bacteria make up one domain by themselves, while Archaea and Eukarya — the domain that includes all plants, fungi, and animals — make up the other two. Bacteria, however, are also the primordial ancestors of all the organisms in the Eukarya domain, including, of course, human animals. The leading evolutionary theory of the kinds of cells that make up these eukaryotes traces their emergence to an endosymbiotic relationship between bacteria. An endosymbiont is any organism that takes up residence in another, which then furnishes it with a nutrient supply and habitat. Over hundreds of millions of years, some bacteria found their way into the bodies of other bacterial species, eventually yielding endosymbiotic relationships so stable that they formed new kinds of life. Bacterial partners in symbiosis swapped genes with each other and, over the course of generations, fused permanently into more complex cellular structures. What were once bacteria living inside others of their kind slowly evolved into specialized subunits like mitochondria, where energy is generated in all eukaryotic cells, and chloroplast, where photosynthesis takes place in plant cells. In this way, bacterial endosymbiosis gave rise to the first single-celled eukaryotes. Their descendants became plants, fungi, and animals.

If bacteria are earth's favorite children, we are all children of bacteria. Products of bacterial society — their living together and within one another — humans, like countless other organisms, now live in a vast but invisible bacterial landscape. And bacteria live in us too. The evolutionary biologist Lynn Margulis, who developed endosymbiotic theory beginning in the late 1960s, wrote accordingly in *Symbiotic Planet* that "each one of us is a massive colony of microorganisms" (1998, 91). The human body makes for such an excellent habitat that humans are, in a way, even more bacterial than they are human. According to a recent study, the average ratio of bacterial cells to human ones is around 1.3 to 1 (Sender, Fuchs, and Milo 2016). An older estimate still cited in popular science media sets the ratio at closer to 10 to 1 for bacteria. Either way, the cellular advantage is on the side of bacteria. Symbiosis continues to be bacteria's preferred mode of social relation, just as it was billions of years ago. While the human organism supplies a myriad of bacterial species with food and housing, these countless tiny residents provide invaluable services in the development and upkeep of their human ecosystem. Among other feats, our bacterial endosymbionts develop and maintain our immune systems, synthesize vitamins while metabolizing otherwise indigestible nutrients, and likely even help regulate mental health.

Of course, it is harder to think so favorably of our ecosystemic entanglements with bacteria when we consider that some of these creatures can make their hosts very ill and can, in fact, kill them. Of the roughly 10,000 species of bacteria that live in humans, only about 100 cause infectious diseases. For most of our species's history, we have had no effective means of combating deadly bacterial infections like typhoid, tuberculosis, and cholera. Due to the threat that these pathogens pose to human populations, until recently, most cultural and scientific interest in bacteria has centered on defeating the nefarious "germ." Today, several decades have passed since penicillin and other antibiotics were made widely available to the public in the 1940s, at least in the so-called developed nations. Considering the diminished threat of bacterial infection in many parts of the world, "good" bacteria are finally getting their due. Initiatives like the Human Microbiome Project, launched by the United States's National Institutes of Health (NIH) in 2007, testify to a growing recognition of the important role that bacteria play in human health. And we need only consider the apparently endless proliferation of probiotic foods and supplements on grocery store shelves to notice that the virtues of bacteria have made their way into everyday life.

At the same time, the chance that some new crop of antibiotic-resistant bacteria may one day plague us looms as a possible threat on the horizon. In this case, we may find the pendulum swinging in the other direction, from bacteriophilia to germ panic. When infectious disease strikes a community, we neglect the fact that we are all bacterial and throw our energy into drawing firm boundaries between us and the microorganic world. This effort, in turn, rebounds onto the macro-scale of human society. As the threat of contagion becomes palpable, we train our anxieties on particular persons, restricting our vision to the human individual rather than the microbial collective that is our species. Efforts to neutralize a microbial threat then morph readily into strategies for controlling and suppressing those human bodies that appear as probable vectors of disease. Historically, the most likely scapegoats have been marginalized groups like immigrants and racial others. At moments of disease outbreak, these populations can function as surrogates for the villainous germ, both in the broader public response and in public health policy.

Racial Contagion

In the late nineteenth century, the world of bacterial pathogens was just emerging as a new site of mass cultural anxiety. The once-dominant miasma theory had attributed disease to environmental factors like foul air and poor hygienic conditions. In the wake of discoveries by legendary bacteriologists like Louis Pasteur and Robert Koch, the germ theory of disease became scientific dogma in the West in the 1890s. In subsequent years, much of the general population of the United States was brought up to speed on the true cause of its ailments, the world of invisible microorganisms that traveled between living hosts in close physical contact. In *The Gospel of Germs*, the historian Nancy Tomes writes that a large swath of us citizens had become "extraordinarily germ conscious" by the end of the nineteenth century (1998, 13). As the germ became a household name, aggressive public health campaigns — waged by newly minted domestic scientists, social workers, and business interests eager to capitalize on the "invention" of the germ — rallied American families to fight their very own sanitary crusades.

Anglo-American cultural production helped raise the alarm. First published in 1926, the American science writer Paul de Kruif's popular history, *The Microbe Hunters*, is an apt expression of the bellicose posture that all good citizens were encouraged to take toward bacteria and other microorganisms, or microbes as they are sometimes called, in the pre-antibiotic era. De Kruif narrates scientific breakthroughs in microbial research as the work of heroic "microbe hunters and death fighters" engaged in battle with a vast army of "immensely small assassins" eager to destroy the human world (1998, 1). Not all writers were as sure as de Kruif, however, that the lines of battle could be so clearly drawn between "humans" on the one side and "microbes" on the other. In his 1894 story, "The Stolen Bacillus," the British writer H.G. Wells points instead to the germ's tendency to amplify divisions in human populations. Wells's story centers on a disgruntled outcast who swipes a vial of *Vibrio cholerae* from a scientist's lab to instigate a cholera epidemic. In so doing, he hopes also to wreak havoc on the reigning social order. Wells assigns his scientist the job of chasing down the aspiring bioterrorist, retrieving the vial, and thus putting a stop to the unholy alliance between dangerous rebel and infectious bacterium.

In the US context, germ panic centered on a population of outsiders whose mere presence threatened to blow up society. In particular, a dominant Anglo-American culture considered the twenty million or so new bodies that arrived in the US between 1880 and 1920 as likely vectors of disease. It is not that these so-called "New Immigrants" were widely regarded as actively plotting bioterrorism like the villain of Wells's story. Rather, they were suspiciously microbial both because their poverty sequestered them in crowded urban slums and, more intangibly, because they seemed so very "foreign." Unlike past immigrant populations, new arrivals from Eastern and Southern Europe, as well as East Asia, did not share in so-called Anglo-Saxon Protestant civilization and thus could not be trusted to abide by its moral hygiene.

At the same time, the media frenzy around disease outbreaks did encourage the general public to regard the "contagious" immigrant as a special kind of criminal. The case of Irish-born cook Mary Mallon, or "Typhoid Mary," as she was dubbed in the papers, was particularly inflammatory (see fig. 1). The first

Fig. 1. Mary Mallon depicted breaking human skulls into a skillet in the June 20, 1909 edition of the *New York American.*

known asymptomatic carrier in America, Mallon unwittingly infected several well-to-do New York families with *Salmonella typhi,* the bacteria responsible for typhoid, before being arrested as a public health menace in 1907 and forced into quarantine. After a legal battle against her imprisonment proved futile, Mallon spent years assuming false identities to evade public health officials before winding up back in quarantine on North Brother Island outside of New York for the rest of her life.

Newspaper coverage of "Typhoid Mary" invariably noted her Irishness, thus helping to solidify the idea of the racialized immigrant, in general, as bearing a criminal affinity with the germ. Another highly publicized outbreak, the so-called San Francisco plague of 1900 to 1904, testifies to the remarkable degree to which legal authorities, spurred by public opinion, were willing to act on this perceived affinity when it proved expedient. A Chinese immigrant known as Chick Gin was the first victim of a bubonic plague epidemic that traveled from Hawaii to San

Francisco aboard a commercial vessel in 1900. Though Chick did not survive his illness, the legal repercussions of his biological intimacy with the plague bacillus *Yersinia pestis* volleyed across the Chinese population of San Francisco. The case of Chick inflamed long-standing anti-Chinese sentiment in California and precipitated an overtly racist quarantine of San Francisco's Chinatown. Only those deemed "white" were allowed to enter and leave, while people of East Asian descent were forcibly sequestered.

Moments of germ panic illuminate how efforts to control the micro-scale of bacterial reproduction also cast into the macro-scale of a political territory. The task of thwarting bacterial reproduction and transmission opens unto newly medicalized modes of suppressing those human bodies that pose an apparent threat to the larger social body. In the United States around 1900, such efforts helped to bulwark Anglo-American hegemony during a period of demographic upheaval that threatened to unsettle the nation's racial and class order. The demonizing of the racialized immigrant at this time, as well as its tendency to shore up Anglo-American power, takes on a particularly cruel irony when considered alongside the longer history of cross-cultural microbial exchange in the Americas. The microbial footprint of the "New Immigrants" was minimal insofar as they did not introduce any new pathogens into the American biosphere. Alternately, British colonists arriving in the seventeenth century did bring with them a host of new bacteria and viruses including those that cause smallpox, bubonic plague, cholera, measles, typhoid, and tuberculosis. Disease outbreaks devastated Indigenous communities in large part because they lacked immunity to European pathogens, thus contributing significantly to Native depopulation during the colonial period. Of all North America's new arrivals, then, it was the ancestors of those later Anglo-American germaphobes who were in fact the most dangerously contagious of all.

The epidemics that Indigenous people suffered in consequence of settler colonialism tragically also helped consolidate British power by clearing North America of many of its Native residents. Disease, however, was not just materially useful to the British, but also served as an ideological tool for shoring up the colonial mission. Indigenous studies scholar Cristobal Silva (2011) shows in *Miraculous Plagues* that disease outbreaks among Indigenous communities served as fodder for British justification narratives throughout the seventeenth century. According to Silva, colonial leaders like John Winthrop, governor of Massachusetts Bay Colony in the 1630s, saw in these epidemics a providential justification of British land claims in North America. As long as Indigenous populations died of smallpox in mass numbers while the British remained comparatively unaffected, Winthrop and his fellow Puritan settlers could regard their colonial project with the satisfaction of a community favored by God.

Colonial-era justification narratives share ideological ground with public health discourse around the "New Immigrants" insofar as both helped Anglo-Americans justify and reinforce their own authority. But those racial others within an Anglo-American order had their own counter-narratives to explain the diseases that plagued them. Some Indigenous people, for instance, made sense of the epidemics that stalked their communities through the depraved character of the British. Writing in the late nineteenth century, Ottawa leader and historian Andrew Blackbird recounts an Indigenous disease narrative from the French and Indian War in his *History of the Ottawa and Chippewa Indians of Michigan*. Blackbird writes that, by the end of the war in 1763, the Ottawa were greatly diminished in number due to the smallpox they had brought back from Montreal during the war. The people of Blackbird's native "Arbor Croche," now Harbor Springs, Michigan, generally maintained that the smallpox was a weaponized disease: it was sent by the British "to kill off the Ottawas and Chippewas because they were friends of the French Government or French King" (Blackbird 1887, 10). The smallpox came packaged in a tin box that was sold to the Ottawa as containing something "supernatural," something that would "do them great good" (9). Upon opening the tin box, the

Ottawa found that it contained a smaller one, which contained a smaller one yet, and so on smaller. Eventually, the Ottawa "came to a very small box, which was not more than an inch long" (9). And in that final box, they discovered "nothing but mouldy particles," which unleashed a "terrible sickness," followed by mass death (10).

Though this history may be apocryphal, there is evidence that the British did in fact weaponize disease for the sake of imperial expansion. In *The Tainted Gift,* Indigenous studies scholar Barbara Alice Mann (2009) examines how British and later US officials exploited Native gift-giving practices to transmit virulent diseases like smallpox to Indigenous populations throughout the eighteenth and nineteenth centuries. At the same time, the story of Native health in the US suggests that quieter strategies of dispossession and willful neglect can be just as effective in facilitating the spread of deadly microbes as purposeful infection. Even within this framework, the Ottawa's "tin box" remains a powerful metaphor. Consider, for instance, the role of residential schools managed by the Bureau of Indian Affairs (BIA) in setting off the tuberculosis crisis that plagued Indigenous populations throughout the twentieth century. Starting in the late nineteenth century, the BIA implemented a policy of taking Native youth, sometimes forcibly, from their homes and sending them to BIA boarding schools. In so doing, the US government hoped to strip children of their Indigenous culture and transform them into proper European-American subjects. This policy of assimilation through education ended up another variation on the Anglo-American gift. Now, the "tin box" was a school, and the "supernatural" thing that it contained, the great boon on offer, was all the moral and practical good that an Indigenous child could secure through a crash course in "civilization."

Woefully underfunded and mismanaged, the BIA residential schools were soon found to be no more than tin boxes of "mouldy particles," and, in particular, *Mycobacterium tuberculosis,* the bacteria that causes tuberculosis. In the first decades of the twentieth century, Native children died of tuberculosis, also known as TB, in startling numbers. What's more, they brought the disease back to their home territories, so that TB soon became the largest health threat facing Indigenous people in the US. While federal inspectors began raising the alarm in the early years of the twentieth century, no serious government effort to address the TB crisis was forthcoming until the 1930s, when President Franklin D. Roosevelt's progressive administration launched an experimental vaccination program targeted at Indigenous communities.

Despite the success of this campaign, historian Christian W. McMillen notes that TB remained the most serious Indigenous health problem into the 1950s. According to McMillen, the persistence of the TB crisis was in no small part a function of the public health establishment's tenacious and faulty conviction that Indigenous people had a genetic susceptibility to infection by *Mycobacterium tuberculosis*. This belief persisted until mid-century despite a growing mountain of scientific evidence against its plausibility, evidence that was available as early as the first decades of the twentieth century. TB is in fact a disease of poverty. The bacteria that cause it flourish in unsanitary, overcrowded living conditions among malnourished people. McMillen suggests that Indigenous racial susceptibility to TB proved such a compelling explanation for public health officials in part because it was convenient in its fatalism. While nothing can be done about genetic risk, addressing poverty requires a costly expenditure of resources. At the same time, the explanation fit within what McMillen identifies as a larger Western narrative about the inability of so-called "primitive" people to "remain in step with modernity" (2008, 609). In this regard, it is a descendant of the colonial-era justification narrative that envisioned Indigenous people as simply disappearing from the North American landscape. More broadly, then, the stubborn epidemiological insistence on Indigenous susceptibility to TB was another variation of the Anglo-American myth that racialized others bear some essential affinity with the germ, now articulated in the language of genetics. Here, as in the case of the "New Immigrants," it functioned to control and indeed expel unruly elements from a hegemonic Anglo-American body politic, contributing to the needless deaths of countless Native people.

The Bacterial Politics of Identity

In *Membranes,* the literary scholar Laura Otis identifies a similar drive towards racialized border control arising in the context of nineteenth-century Western imperialism as it developed alongside both germ theory and modern understandings of the biological cell. Otis suggests that anxieties around contagion, and indeed foreign penetration that political expansion itself exacerbated, gave rise to a new mode of conceiving self and nation in terms of exclusion and the strict enforcement of borders in both Europe and the US. This "membrane model" of identity takes its metaphorical cue from the cellular membrane, which defends the interior of a cell from its surrounding environment (1999, 3). The model bases identity, whether personal or social, on the capacity for expanding one's boundaries, while also vehemently keeping out external forces.

Otis ends *Membranes* with the wish that the biological sciences may one day "serve a new ideology celebrating global interconnections" rather than helping imperialistic cultures shore up their "fears of invasion," as did these earlier developments in bacteriology and cell theory (174). Margulis's endosymbiotic theory of cellular evolution does just that. Margulis instructs us that complex life did not originate in the strict enforcement of borders, but in the tendency of bacteria to make homes in the bodies of strangers and to permit others to do the same to them. The ongoing dependence of countless species on symbiotic alliances with bacteria further testifies to the folly of conceiving organisms as strictly bounded individuals. The Hawaiian bobtail squid, for instance, only develops its distinctive luminescent glow with the help of the bacteria, *Vibrio fischeri,* which colonize it shortly after birth. In exchange for a habitat and nutrient supply, *V. fischeri* hides the squid from predators by illuminating it, thus concealing its silhouette and helping it blend in

Fig. 2. The Hawaiian bobtail squid (*Euprymna scolopes*) swims in the shallow sand flats of the Hawaiian archipelago, illuminated by its endosymbiont, *V. fischeri.*

with its surroundings (see fig. 2). Or consider the stomach of cattle, which coevolved with a variety of bacterial species that help it digest grass. Rumen, one of four chambers in the bovine stomach, is essentially a fermentation chamber full of bacteria that breaks down the fibrous cellulose in grass. If we remember our own human dependence on bacteria, we may be tempted to shake off the notion of individuality altogether and recognize ourselves, along with all life, simply as so many nodes in a vast network of symbiotic alliances.

And yet bacteria push us to go further in dismantling the individual than even a proper consideration of symbiosis. Symbiosis presumes a relationship *between* distinct organisms and thus retains some concept of exclusive identity. Alternatively, no bacterium was ever an individual in the first place. Each is a copy of another of its kind, and each split itself in two to make more copies. Bacteria reproduce by binary fission, so that a bacterium spawns offspring by dividing its single cell into two nearly identical offspring. While reproductive rates vary across species, *E. Coli,* for instance, typically divides every twenty minutes. More so, bacteria's amazing persistence and ubiquity on earth depends on their readiness to both incorporate and fuse into their environs. Bacteria's evolutionary success comes from what American writer Arno Karlen, in his *Biography of a Germ,* calls the "constant buzz of genetic traffic within and between microbes" (2001, 84). Bacteria can absorb floating fragments of DNA from their surroundings and from each other, thus acquiring new traits like increased immunity or virulence. And they shed genetic material readily, as if eager to disrupt their own "oneness" further: in a process called conjugation, a donor bacterium extends a bridge-like tube called a pilus in order to transfer DNA to a waiting recipient bacterium.

If we are to glean a model of individuality from bacteria, then, it ought to be predicated on a radical sociality that permeates, ruptures, and transforms "individuals" constantly, so that the *one* always slips into the *collective.* It might be difficult to think in this way, especially from within our contemporary US ideological climate, which, at least in its dominant form, suspects most efforts at collective action or socialized care of dangerous political extremism. We may likewise be discouraged by the xenophobic, racist, and classist politics that have been central to the history of Anglo-American dealings with bacteria in the US. But humans are descendants of bacteria and may take hold of this inheritance yet, both in thought and in politics. Having never left the age of bacteria, we can think with them towards a new politics of collective identity for the human and more-than-human social. As we make our leap towards the collective, we may be heartened to imagine the countless friendly bacteria that help constitute our bodies and our earth cheering us on.

References and Further Reading

Amyes, Sebastian G.B. 2013. *Bacteria: A Very Short Introduction.* Oxford: Oxford University Press.

Blackbird, Andrew J. 1887. *History of the Ottawa and Chippewa Indians of Michigan: A Grammar of Their Language, and Personal and Family History of the Author.* Ypsilanti: The Ypsilantian Job Printing House.

Dejong, David H. 2007. "'Unless They Are Kept Alive': Federal Indian Schools and Student Health, 1878–1918." *American Indian Quarterly* 31, no. 2: 256–82. https://www.jstor.org/stable/4138947.

Gilbert, Scott F., Jan Sapp, and Alfred I. Tauber. 2012. "A Symbiotic View of Life: We Have Never Been Individuals." *The Quarterly Review of Biology* 87, no. 4: 325–41. DOI: 10.1086/668166.

Karlen, Arno. 2001. *Biography of a Germ.* New York: Anchor Books.

Kraut, Alan M. 1994. *Silent Travelers: Germs, Genes, and the "Immigrant Menace."* Baltimore: The Johns Hopkins University Press.

Kruif, Paul de. 1996. *The Microbe Hunters.* New York: Harcourt.

Margulis, Lynn. 1998. *Symbiotic Planet: A New Look at Evolution.* New York: Basic Books.

Margulis, Lynn, and Dorion Sagan. 1997. *Microcosmos: Four Billion Years of Microbial Evolution.* Berkeley: University of California Press.

Mann, Barbara Alice. 2009. *The Tainted Gift: The Disease Method of Frontier Expansion.* Santa Barbara: Praeger.

McMillen, Christian W. 2008. "'The Red Man and the White Plague': Rethinking Race, Tuberculosis, and American Indians, ca. 1890–1950." *Bulletin of the History of Medicine* 82, no. 3: 608–45. http://www.jstor.org/stable/44448614.

Otis, Laura. 1999. *Membranes: Metaphors of Invasion in Nineteenth-Century Literature, Science, and Politics.* Baltimore: Johns Hopkins University Press.

Sender, Ron, Shai Fuchs, and Ron Milo. 2016. "Revised Estimates for the Number of Human and Bacteria Cells in the Body." *PLoS Biology* 14, no. 8: e1002533. DOI: 10.1371/journal.pbio.1002533.

Silva, Cristobal. 2011. *Miraculous Plagues: An Epidemiology of Early New England Narrative.* Oxford: Oxford University Press.

Tomes, Nancy. 1998. *The Gospel of Germs: Men, Women, and the Microbe in American Life.* Cambridge: Harvard University Press.

Wald, Priscilla. 2008. *Contagious: Cultures, Carriers, and the Outbreak Narrative.* Durham: Duke University Press.

Wells, H.G. 1894. "The Stolen Bacillus." *Pall Mall Budget,* June 21.

CHAPTER 3

Corals

Damien Bright

Corals make their way into the world as diminutive specks of life. In time, they combine to build monumental reefs that boast improbable shapes and patterns, radiate a festival of color, and support myriad creatures from parrot fish to manta rays, deep-water eels to green turtles. As an expression of abundant nature, coral is inventive and resourceful, singular and collaborative. Global tourism and media industries channel these qualities when depicting tropical reefscapes as timeless escapes from the drudgery of modern living. Disney's clownfish Nemo, for instance, abandons the sanitized confines of the dentist's aquarium and, in a daring flight across the Great Barrier Reef, finds home. Such associations, however fanciful, lend urgency and gravity to reports that climate disruption is unraveling coral biology and with it the very fabric of ocean life. This prospect not only exposes communities who live and depend on reefs, it also strains the planet as humans know it. Today, coral ambivalently evokes forces of creation and destruction.

Fig. 1. A variety of corals form an outcrop on Flynn Reef, part of the Great Barrier Reef near Cairns, Queensland, Australia. Image taken by Toby Hudson. CC BY-SA 3.0.

A Measure of the Living Oceans

From the standpoint of biology, corals are a group of marine invertebrates that thrive in tropical and semi-tropical waters, although lesser-studied deep-sea corals exist at all latitudes. The oldest coral fossils date back to the Cambrian period, some 540 million years ago, but specimens biologically related to today's corals dominate the geological record from the mid-Triassic, 250 million years ago. Currently, there are nearly six thousand documented species of coral, roughly separated into "soft" and "hard" kinds. Hard corals extrude a stony skeleton of calcium carbonate at their base, and some form plates and others make ruffles, boulders, or branches. Near the surface their bodies elaborate a reef's patchwork structure, and at depth their skeletons compress to make its limestone foundation. Soft corals do not lay down a calcareous skeleton but embellish reefs or other submerged structures such as fans, whips, bushes, and grasses (see fig. 1).

All corals are sedentary animals that begin life as polyps a few millimeters in diameter and attach to surfaces with their mineral-rich base. Their bodies are composed of digestive and reproductive organs. At the top is an opening to draw food in and out, ringed with stinging tentacles called nematocysts that stun microorganisms and fend off encroaching neighbors. Most corals live as a so-called colony, a collection of genetically identical polyps with a shared metabolism that forms through asexual reproduction. Single polyps divide or bud new versions of themselves to grow a larger structure, connected via a tissue matrix, which in some cases can weigh in at multiple tons. But corals can also reproduce sexually, either by releasing sperm and egg bundles that fertilize in the water column or "brooding" offspring internally and releasing them as larvae. Some offspring settle besides their parents, while currents carry others away, perhaps to a nearby rock, sponge, or human-made structure, perhaps to an adjacent reef, to open water, or into a predator's mouth.

Like many animals, a variety of beneficial bacteria and fungi colonize corals and keep them alive. More distinctively, the vast majority of tropical reef-building corals bond with plants, a family of marine algae called "zooxanthellae." Zooxanthellae take up residence in the stomach cells of a coral host in a mutually beneficial arrangement known as endosymbiosis. The algae use sunlight to photosynthesize, processing coral waste and producing energy, which dramatically increases the rate of coral and thus reef growth. The relationship also explains coral's many hues: coral flesh is clear but, when filled with algae, can flush deep green, tawny brown, burnt umber, blood red, and so on. Together, coral animal and algal plant breathe, feed, and multiply at a scale and pace that would be impossible by themselves.

Time and place mark coral skeletons, making them a living measure of their milieu. Although corals cover less than one percent of the earth's surface, over 25 percent of all marine animals depend on reefs. These habitats have long been likened to rain forests, nurseries, or cities due to the communities they support, from flocks of birds to bales of turtles, from casts of crabs to tufts of turf algae. This arrangement is dynamic, and coral itself is conditioned by the organisms it sustains. Wave friction, pressure changes, storm impacts, the daily deeds of untold lives — all of these shape patterns of coral growth and decline. This holds locally (how a single coral colony forms a patch of reef) and globally (how entire reef systems form in the ocean), with ripple effects on plants, algae, fish, birds, and hence also dependent human communities. Reefs sustain food webs and migration routes, ring islands with shelter, and protect coastlines. Thus, corals are powerful "sentinels" of environmental change, to borrow a term from social scientists Frédéric Keck and Andrew Lakoff. Like growth rings in tree trunks, corals record ambient conditions in their skeletons, from which scientists extract coral cores for analysis. In recent decades, they have demonstrated the mounting stress of runaway global warming.

Corals can accommodate seasonal fluctuations in light, temperature, and flow, along with occasional impacts from storms, agricultural runoff, boating accidents, fishing, or coastal development. However, the scale and pace of the climate crisis is multiplying these changes to the point of exceeding coral's adaptive abilities. Because they cannot regulate their body temperature, rising ocean temperatures compromise the metabolic processes of corals. What's more, as carbon dioxide concentrations increase in the ocean, so does acidity, which reduces the number of carbonates available for corals to build skeletons and compromises reef integrity. Added to this, the relationship between coral hosts and their endosymbiotic zooxanthellae is shifting from beneficial to toxic. With higher temperatures and light levels, the latter begin producing more oxygen than the former can consume. Corals then jettison their zooxanthellae into the water column and take their chances with a drastically reduced food and energy supply. A potentially fatal stress response, this micro-phenomenon is visible at the macro-scale as "coral bleaching." Without zooxanthellae, corals lose color and expose their underlying mineral skeleton, hence the expression. Once localized and occasional, bleaching has intensified in the last two centuries. Instead of occurring every twenty years, it now happens twice in a decade, sometimes year after year, and affects ever more corals on a given reef and more reefs in the oceans. The human equivalent of these symptoms of climatic stress would be heat stroke, brittle bones, and shortness of breath, all increasingly chronic, acute, and contagious.

As hermit crabs, humpback whales, reef herons, and, indeed, human beings depend on corals, these tiny creatures are living proof for contemporary descriptions of all life on earth as bound together in a tenuous, if not terminal, compact. Understanding corals this way can produce a profoundly anxious worldview. In *Coral Whisperers,* social scientist Irus Braverman (2018) interviews and observes coral scientists today and shows how they live, in her words, "on the brink" with the corals they study, oscillating between hope and despair. Some view their work as testimony to urge political transformation and others as diagnosis to urge experimental intervention. These differences in approach are a reminder that the questions and methods that scientists pursue draw on and draw out cultural attitudes and political values.

The vast geographic spread of coral makes it central to a diversity of traditions past and enduring, from ancient Egyptian burial rites to Polynesian creation stories and international commerce in Southeast Asia before, during, and after colonization. But it is the so-called Western tradition, in achieving global hegemony, that is uniquely responsible for the dominant understandings of nature that precipitated and continue to drive the climate crisis. A closer look at the place of corals within Anglo-European philosophies of nature shows that coral and nature more broadly take divergent meanings and uses within the development of Western thought. This history of disagreement over what coral is and why it matters helps us challenge a major, albeit contested claim of the Western tradition that its modes of knowledge and action spring from a self-consistent, definitive, and total account of worldly reality and good conduct therein.

The Many Lives of Coral within the Western Tradition

Humanists and social scientists have long queried a human tendency to understand the world by sorting things into categories and classifications, of which biology is one expression. Conspicuously ambiguous things like coral — an admixture of animal, plant, and mineral — often complicate this activity. When naturalists, poets, and ordinary people puzzle over these seeming oddities, they often appeal to circulating assumptions about how the world hangs together. Coral is therefore a useful guide to questioning the historical distinctions between classical, early modern, and modern ideas of nature writ large in the Western tradition.

Coral cuts an unusual figure within the classical worldview. This idea of nature, as we find it articulated most forcefully in Aristotelian philosophy, presupposes that everything that exists has an inner principle: plants can grow; animals can grow, move, and sense; humans can grow, move, sense, and think. In striving to do these things well, all seek to express their own inner principle and thus the principle of the universe. How, then, to make sense of a mixture of these categories? Red or precious coral, a group of organisms now attributed to the genus *Corallium,* was widespread throughout the Mediterranean and garnered commercial, medicinal, and literary attention. Ovid's *Metamorphoses* offers one origin story. When the hero Perseus vanquishes Medusa, a mythical creature with venomous snakes for hair whose gaze turns its subjects to stone, he lays her head on a bed of seagrass. Upon contact, the serpentine and petrifying qualities of Medusa's head combine with the aquatic plant, and red coral comes into being. This thing of bone, branch, and blood delights nearby nymphs, who sow it throughout the surrounding seas. This transformation myth explains coral as a mixed but stable entity in intimate connection with cosmic forces. The harder, curlier, and redder the coral harvested at sea,

Fig. 2. Portrait of a young boy with red coral teething beads in 1625. Unknown painter, Flemish school, ca. 1620–30.

the greater its striving to express "coralness," an unlikely yet un-disputable combination of mineral strength, plant growth, and animal movement.

The category-defying complexity of coral helps explain its prominent role in antiquity. As bone, branch, and blood were tropes of vitality and endurance, so coral featured in art and handicraft, pharmaceutical and philosophical treatises, along with folklore and religious worship. Historian Shannon Kelley (2014) explains that naturalists, healers, and poets from ancient Greece through to the late sixteenth century lauded coral's pow-er to soothe pain, stanch bleeding, quench fever, help teething, grow orchards, sprout gardens, scatter storms, calm winds, lift melancholy, and inspire romantic love. Newborns wore coral jewelry for patience, farmers used coral tinctures for luck, and lovers cast coral charms for nerve. These qualities are, of course, human, not coralline, and they correspond to ways that people, not corals, overcome difficulty. As a tangible display of something expressing its Aristotelian inner principle, coral provided people in tough times with a touchstone for summoning the determination needed to go on. Coral was no miracle cure but could urge clarity. For some, this may have meant magical thinking akin to a placebo effect, others may have found succor in picturing an example to emulate, and some may simply have lauded coral out of habit or social convention.

This wide range of uses helps explain the great demand for coral as well as the Mediterranean industry of coral collection and trade that grew to accommodate it. While wealthy elites claimed the most expressive examples, lower-grade varieties circulated widely, as did fakes and facsimiles. As new harvesting techniques and trade routes emerging in the fourteenth through sixteenth century began to deplete red coral from Florence to Tunis, coral demand came to play a crucial role in the growth of maritime networks. Despite its increasing rarity, coral persisted within Western healing practices. For instance, one seventeenth-century Flemish painting (see fig. 2) shows a well-to-do child in embroidered finery, with holstered sword, holding a trained bird on a perch with a dog lying patiently at his feet, while a set of red coral teething bracelets and necklace bedazzle his wrists and chest. The unknown identities of painter and child confirm red coral's ready appeal as a companion to health and wealth.

In the early modern view of nature, the properties and qualities of the observable world reflected the creative powers of a divine maker whose wisdom only human reasoning could appreciate. Rather than expressing its inner principle, coral was one component among others within a world mechanism designed with clockwork precision by a divine external observer. This idea of nature developed in tandem with the so-called Scientific Revolution of the sixteenth century when new techniques of calculation, instrumentation, and experimentation transformed the aim, scope, and applications of science, medicine, industry, art, architecture, and commerce. In studying nature as a mechanical puzzle, scholars of this period sorted its "pieces" by size, shape, form, and function through drawing, dissection, and manipulation. By the eighteenth century, they had grouped corals with river polyps, sponges, mussels, and sea worms as so many "zoophytes," or plant-like animals. What corals lost in cosmic significance they gained in interest for a new natural history that asked why some of nature's smallest creatures took such ambiguous forms. So, although corals were called "sea insects" and deemed "low" within an imagined divine order of things, scholars earned high praise for their study. Consider William Herschel, who developed the microscope with his sister Caroline Herschel. When Herschel made his debut at the Bath Philosophical Society in 1780, he bolstered his reputation and "his" invention's merits by selecting a subject beyond his usual interests yet sure to woo his audience: the growth and measurement of "corallines."

As Western ideas about corals and micro-life shifted from the sixteenth century onwards, so did ideas about coral's macro-form, namely the coral reef. In a period marked by the tight connection between global maritime navigation and domestic power struggles, reefs also became trials of human reasoning for economic and political actors. Unlike the "soft" red coral of the Mediterranean, the hitherto unmet "hard" tropical reef-building corals of the Atlantic, Pacific, and Indian oceans formed vast submerged structures that imperiled the would-be "conquest" of the high seas. Royal, commercial, and popular investments in trade, smuggling, and enslavement led to countless shipwrecks. As the loss of life and cargo changed how people saw reefs, it also changed how people used them.

Historian of finance François Ewald explains that Renaissance merchant guilds named the foundational concept of insurance, "risk," after the early modern Italian for reef, "risco." In the parlance of insurance, a risk is not just any old danger.

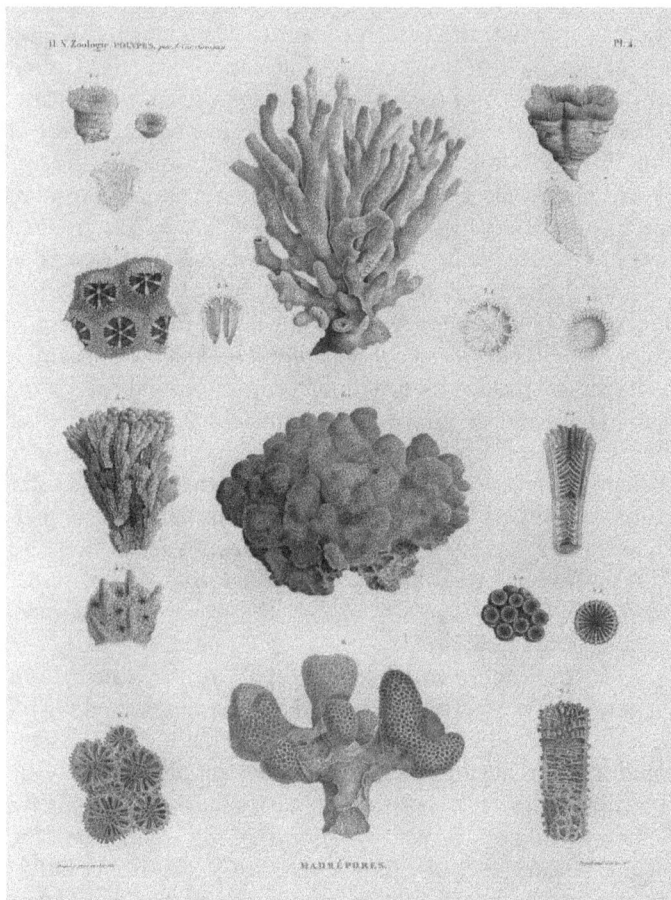

Fig. 3. Coral engravings from the *Description of Egypt,* multi-authored set of volumes published between 1809 and 1829 to record and reenact Napoleon's so-called expedition to Egypt.

It is one you cannot see but whose likelihood you can predict and therefore wager on. In equating reefs with risks, Europeans once again looked to coral to face uncertainty — this time not as a cosmic companion but as a fearsome riddle, practical and metaphorical, apt to test human ingenuity. Thus, in his 1513 treatise *The Prince,* the Italian humanist Niccolò Machiavelli uses reefs as an analogy for a likely yet hidden obstacle to power: the contempt of rivals, plotters, and subjects. By picturing reefs as conspirators and conspirators as reefs, Machiavelli urges his reader to imagine that wielding authority is less a matter of natural ability or divine right than a cunning display of reasoning in the face of the unknown. One devoted reader, the French emperor Napoleon Bonaparte, made a system and a spectacle of this method during his 1798 invasion of Egypt when he drafted an army of linguists, geographers, historians, and naturalists to subject the people and places of the fetishized "Orient" to European know-how. Corals figured among the many images circulated to impress metropolitan audiences with the authority and reach of the Western gaze (see fig. 3).

Coral continued to preoccupy political and scientific authorities into the nineteenth century. For instance, British Royal Navy officers and Royal Society naturalists working together hand in glove were able to establish, but could not explain, the connection between coral biology and reef geology. There were immediate strategic implications. Could corals make reefs so quickly that maps made for one journey would prove useless for the next? The dilemma circulated widely in naturalists' papers, travelers' tales, and illustrators' images. In his debut monograph of 1842, *The Structure and Distribution of Coral Reefs,* Charles Darwin ventured a bold hypothesis. If there were mountains and valleys in the ocean as there are on land, then tiny corals might build reefs layer by layer on bedrock that sank slowly into the sea. Further, if these building and sinking actions were constant, gradual, and coordinated enough, then corals would sustain a robust reef near the surface that could supplant the land mass as it slipped from view. Darwin's explanation of the scalar jump from coral to reef reflects an emerging modern understanding that nature is not a mechanism of fixed design but a dynamic mesh of organisms that live, grow, and die in a given time and place, thereby altering the conditions by which other things live, grow, and die around, and after, them.

Darwin weaved his coral theory together from imperial orders, scientific institutions, sailors' know-how, and in-situ observations, as historian Alistair Sponsel (2018) explains in *Darwin's Evolving Identity*. Between the lines of Darwin's idea lay a provocative speculation, that is, that the earth did not simply contain many life histories but had a life history of its own. While this history's rhythm and tempo may defy direct observation with human senses, even when augmented by microscopes, its conditions and limits remained measurable, such as the rate at which the seafloor sinks or at which corals build. This made Darwin's theory testable, albeit with difficulty. For instance, if geologists drilled the right hole in the right reef, they could extract a core of coral from the surface to the bedrock. "Coring" thus became a centerpiece of coral science, requiring vast resources and technical proficiency. The ultimate test that Darwin imagined for his theory only happened in 1952 when, as part of a survey of the effects of atomic weaponry on marine life, us Navy divers drilled a nearly 5,000-foot coral core and indeed hit bedrock.

With evidence that corals grew reefs too slowly to threaten imperial expansion, Western powers devised ways of putting coral into their service. In the modern view, if nature was alive and its different forms adapted to a given place, then these could be identified, cultivated, and "improved" the better to grow metropolitan wealth and secure colonial settlement. From the early nineteenth century, for example, state and commercial enterprises raided Australian reefs, taking turtles for meat, pearl shell for buttons, and sea cucumbers for trade. Historians Ben Daley and Peter Griggs (2006) document the largely forgotten history of mining for phosphate, guano, and lime to develop the sugar cane industry inland of the Great Barrier Reef. These varied projects disrupted spiritual and political bonds that connect First Nations with coral reefs and conscripted residents of the region, including colonized subjects from neighboring countries to a settler colonial Australia in which nature is something to claim and domesticate in the name of "civilization."

Throughout the nineteenth century, corals circulated largely within the Western world as representations, whether colorful drawings, adventure tales, sculptural curios or, by century's end, photographs. Cultural historian Ann Elias (2019) explains in *Coral Empire* how the new medium of underwater photography used colonized subjects and industrial diving technology to produce elaborately staged images of a "hidden" world teeming with "unknown" life. From the 1920s, these images graced newspapers, museum exhibits, and artworks to present nature as alive, untamed, and "primitive," yet ripe for domestication through modern media technologies. Literary scholar Michelle Elleray (2011) documents a quieter but no less powerful example of the social force of such representations, where Victorian children's literature borrowed from natural science to celebrate corals as "little builders" of vast ocean worlds, a metaphor that became the centerpiece of evangelical periodicals encouraging working children to donate their wages to build children's missions in the Pacific. These religious tracts turned the everyday struggles of imperial subjects at home, missionized subjects abroad, and reef-building Pacific corals into a fantastical coming-of-age story of industrious self-improvement. For aspiring naturalists or paranoid sovereigns in the early modern period, ambiguous corals and forbidding reefs may have been "good to think with," to borrow anthropologist Claude Lévi-Strauss's (1962) felicitous expression. In the modern era, they became material and symbolic resources for imperial forces as they conscripted mass publics to produce a new historical and moral world order.

Coral-Human Relations, Between Past and Future

As a guide to Western natural histories, coral induces something like vertigo. In antiquity, each shard of red coral opened the door to a cosmic order of inner principles. For the early moderns, the coralline "sea insect" was lowly matter in the grand scheme of things, but a cunning match for human reason. And in the nineteenth and twentieth centuries, the tropical coral polyp's living labor built reef worlds that archived earth's deep history and rationalized the barbarity of imperialism. These are dizzying shifts in scale and relationality, each illustrating a different conception of the observable world. Such ideas do not change all at once nor without continuities and myriad exceptions, resistances, and minoritarian currents.

Coral offers a tangible expression of how tenuous arrangements at the smallest scale give rise to the extraordinarily complex phenomena we observe and encounter in the world. As a figure that not only dwells in the oceans but brings them to life, coral highlights the limits to what human beings can know of and do within the natural world to which, nonetheless, we belong. Accordingly, even as coral crystallizes different ways of seeing nature and why it matters, it also shows how these ideas shift over time in contributing to Western aspirations to global hegemony. Such contributions are not metaphorical: coral has been named, renamed, collected, traded, stolen, copied, pulverized, drilled, mapped, dissected, sculpted, sketched, photographed, mythologized, sermonized, romanticized, demonized, and eulogized. These human actions are so many ways that people have embedded the micro-macro labors of reef-building corals within economic, political, and moral projects that have shaped human history. Put directly, although corals may have one planetary story, since people have been around, they have known many histories.

One such history unfolds today, where the decline of coral reefs often takes center stage in discussions of the climate crisis. Yet, while coral bleaching is increasingly prevalent, it is no newcomer to the geological record. The earth's prior five mass extinctions all coincide with "reef gaps," protracted periods in which reef-building lifeforms are entirely absent from the fossil record following changes in global ocean chemistry similar to those at work today. This makes cumulative bleaching events nothing short of an omen. Insofar as they register the scale of

planetary change underway, corals show the intimate bond between their micro-lives, human history, and our future together.
Indeed, while what ails today's corals is biogeochemical dysreg-
ulation, one thing causing this is the human appetite for their
forebears, namely, generations of reef-building invertebrates,
their die-out marking prior mass extinctions and their decom-
posed bodies constituting vast oil reserves that are drilled, de-
pleted, refined, transported, and combusted every minute of
the day. If the climate crisis shows that global society neglects
coral at its own peril, then imagining a less toxic future requires
questioning the underlying ideas and values that make human
collectivity and its maintenance, even in the most devastating
configurations, impossible without coral.

An influential view among environmental studies scholars
is that corals themselves offer lessons in compassion and justice that can check the rapacious forces driving global warming. Corals make home and kin across species boundaries and
national borders. They rely not on self-interest but mutual de-
pendency to generate abundance, growth, and change. Corals
thereby demonstrate that cooperation, not dominance, holds
life together. Accordingly, policy makers, economists, and non-
governmental organizations (NGOs) diminish what coral reefs,
and people, can be by treating them not as beloved and respect-
ed kin but as a means to short-term human ends (e.g., tourism,
fishing, research, national borders, awareness campaigns). So
too, future abundance would require breaking open the hegemony of Western thought to welcome understandings of nature
and communal living from Indigenous and non-Western traditions. More than a physical archive of earth's deep history, coral
is a powerful guide for tracking, contrasting, and challenging
the human and more-than-human agreements that have made
the historical present, some creative, many destructive, some to
celebrate, many to atone for, some to hold onto, and many to
surrender once and for all.

References and Further Reading

Braverman, Irus. 2018. *Coral Whisperers: Scientists on the Brink.* Berkeley: University of California Press.

Collingwood, R.G. 1945. *The Idea of Nature.* Oxford: The Clarendon Press.

"Coral Tutorial." n.d. *National Ocean Service.* https://oceanservice.noaa.gov/education/tutorial_corals/welcome.html.

Daley, Ben, and Peter Griggs. 2006. "Mining the Reefs and Cays: Coral, Guano and Rock Phosphate Extraction in the Great Barrier Reef, Australia, 1844–1940." *Environment and History* 12, no. 4: 395–433. https://www.jstor.org/stable/20723590.

Darwin, Charles. 1842. *The Structure and Distribution of Coral Reefs.* London: Smith, Elder and Co.

Elias, Ann. 2019. *Coral Empire: Underwater Oceans, Colonial Tropics, Visual Modernity.* Durham: Duke University Press.

Elleray, Michelle. 2011. "Little Builders: Coral Insects, Missionary Culture, and the Victorian Child." *Victorian Literature and Culture* 39, no. 1: 223–38. DOI: 10.1017/S1060150310000367.

Ewald, François. "Insurance and Risk." In *The Foucault Effect: Studies in Governmentality,* edited by Graham Burchell, Colin Gordon, and Peter Miller, 197–210. Chicago: University of Chicago Press, 1991.

Kelley, Shannon. 2014. "The King's Coral Body: A Natural History of Coral and the Post-tragic Ecology of *The Tempest.*" *Journal for Early Modern Cultural Studies* 14, no. 1: 115–42. https://www.jstor.org/stable/jearlmodcultstud.14.1.115.

Lakoff, Andrew, and Frédéric Keck. 2013. "Preface: Sentinel Devices." *Limn* 1, no. 3: 2–3. https://limn.it/articles/preface-sentinel-devices-2/.

Lévi-Strauss, Claude. 1962. *Totemism.* Translated by Rodney Needham. London: Merlin Press.

Sponsel, Alistair. 2018. *Darwin's Evolving Identity: Adventure, Ambition, and the Sin of Speculation.* Chicago: University of Chicago Press.

Veron, J.E.N. 2007. *A Reef in Time: The Great Barrier Reef from Beginning to End.* Cambridge: The Belknap Press of Harvard University Press.

CHAPTER 4

Fungi

Karen Leona Anderson

"How puzzling all these changes are! I'm never sure what I'm going to be, from one minute to another!" says Alice as she nibbles a mushroom in *Alice's Adventures in Wonderland* (Caroll 1865, 74). Her bemusement is typical of the human reaction to fungi: as an organism neither plant nor animal, living at both micro and macro scales, and appearing abruptly and unpredictably in a bewildering array of forms, fungi have long resisted human classificatory schemas and physical control. How Anglo-American culture has interpreted that resistance — as a grotesque threat or as a model for admirable resilience — has changed over the twentieth and twenty-first centuries as political, economic, and environmental changes have emphasized our radical dependence on these shapeshifters.

Increasingly, too, our scientific and cultural attention has focused on micro-fungi. While fungi are still best known by their macroscopic fruiting bodies, or "mushrooms," they exist as micro-matter in the form of spores, unicellular fungi such as yeast, and in the microscopic filaments called hyphae that together constitute the mycelium, or underground part, of the fungus. Most fungal bodies develop, invisibly, as hyphae: these tube-like structures, which grow at their tips to create a dense mat called the mycelium, go on to take a bewildering array of visible incarnations, from classic gilled "toadstools" to black mold blooms.

The ability of fungi to shift from micro to macro has had a significant effect on human life: they are a major cause of hunger because they destroy crop plants and constitute one of the most dangerous and uncontrollable human pathogens; they are the basis of bread, beer, wine, penicillin, and the production of some hormones and vaccines. Their mycelial networks help sustain plant life on the planet, and thus, our own. They can resist and perhaps draw energy from radiation, as we know from their appearance at toxic sites such as Hiroshima and Chernobyl; they survive in space; and, together, microscopic hyphae constitute what is arguably the largest and oldest living organism in underground honey fungus that is over two thousand acres wide in Oregon. Although over 100,000 kinds of fungi have been identified, this is believed to be only a tiny fraction of existing fungal species.

The story of fungi in human culture can also be read as a story of quicksilver scale-shifting, ever frustrating our attempts to divide the world neatly into micro and macro, visible and invisible, individual and collective. Even at the level of taxonomy, fungi have posed difficult problems. Neither plant nor animal, they nevertheless share characteristics of both, remaining sessile like plants but, like animals, operating as digesters rather than producers of their own food. Early European taxonomic work on mushrooms hinged on edibility and toxicity. Later, in work by Pier Antonio Micheli and early microscopist Robert Hooke, seventeenth-century scientific attention to micro-matter led to the identification of spores and hyphae and established a crucial link between hyphal structures and macroscopic mushrooms. Carl Linnaeus classified fungi in the genus *Chaos* within the family of worms, and Hooke described them as a kind of sponge — an interesting choice in light of recent genetic work that shows that fungi are closer to animals than plants.

While the eighteenth- and nineteenth-century reassessment of fungi as plants and their subsequent classifications relied heavily on morphological differences, twentieth- and twenty-first century mycology has focused on the interrelations between fungi and other organisms. With the rise of microbiology, genetics, and ecology, gene sequencing has allowed mycologists to group fungi according to evolutionary history rather than physical form. Since the late 1990s, scientists have also sought to understand the "wood wide web," or the ecology of forests with a focus on fungal roles, by mapping mycorrhizal connections between fungi and the roots of plants that allow for the transfer of nutrients, carbon, and information. Fungi have been shown to live as mutualists with trees and insects, as symbionts in organisms such as lichens, as pathogens, and as independent organisms — often interchangeably as conditions shift. They sustain forest life by breaking down dead plant matter as saprophytes; they live in and on plant roots as mutualists, trading soil-extracted nutrients for sugars and fatty acids; they live between plant cells as endophytes; and, as necessary, they become parasites if the organisms they live near, on, or in, weaken.

Culturally, fungi's changeability in size and form has been understood in the Anglo-American context as fascinating, bewildering, frightening, and grotesque. Fungi have been seen as alien organisms defying categorization, as toxic pests or weeds, as poisonous foods or risky medicines, as signs of mysterious ruin and decay, and as vestiges of uncontrollable magic, otherworldliness, or spiritual essence. Some outliers exist: Erasmus Darwin's view of the truffle in his *Loves of the Plants* (1789) is uncharacteristically sunny, for example. However, as R.T. Rolfe (1974, 18) demonstrates in his influential study *The Romance of the Fungus World,* most instances of fungi in canonical writing — from at least Percy Bysshe Shelly's "pale, fleshy" fungi in his poem, "The Sensitive Plant" from 1820 — have invoked a sense of ruin, decay, and death.

More specifically, British and American writers from the nineteenth century were generally "mycophobic," a term developed by ethnomycologists R. Gordon Wasson and Valentina Guercken (1957) to describe a hatred or fear of fungi. They also

"I WAS IN A FOREST OF COLOSSAL FUNGI."

Fig. 1. An image from John Uri Lloyd's fantasy novel *Etidorhpa* (1895) that illustrates the scale-shifting fungal imagination.

tended to be micro-phobic. As Rolfe notes, Charles Dickens, Alfred Lord Tennyson, and Henry Wadsworth Longfellow all used fungi as figurative shorthand for degenerative conditions arising from an invisible cause. Charles Chesnutt describes these as "growths, social as well as vegetable, which flourish best in the dark" (Rolfe and Rolfe 2014, 281). Even the towering fungal forests of the fantasy writing of the nineteenth century, such as Jules Verne's (1871) *Journey to the Center of the Earth* and John Uri Lloyd's (1895) *Etidorhpa,* associate fungi with darkness, rankness, and oddity (see fig. 1). Lewis Carroll, in Alice's celebrated encounter with the caterpillar, linked mushrooms with magical, radical, and sometimes threatening changes in size and shape.

Though spores had been identified in the eighteenth century and hyphae observed in the seventeenth, fungal micro-matter was still little understood by the nineteenth century. It was also suspected as being an important source of human disease and destruction. As Sari Altschuler (2018) notes, the 1845 version of Edgar Allan Poe's story "The Fall of the House of Usher" provides a particularly clear and striking example of this type of micro-mycophobia. Altschuler theorizes that Poe's story coevolved with a medical hypothesis, proposed by his physician-poet friend John Kearsley Mitchell, that cholera was caused by fungal spores. As Altschuler shows, Poe's fungal imagery intensified as he revised the story, highlighting the "minute fungi [overspreading] the whole exterior" of the doomed house (Poe 1845, 149). This intensification was likely both influenced by and influential in Mitchell's gothic, xenophobic medical understanding of fungal spores as developing from an "almost invisible cell" to a cloud of spores "so minute as to look like smoke as they rose in the air" (Mitchell 1859, 41). For Mitchell, the fungal spore became a "foreign intruder [...] welcomed by a domestic facilitation," and "enter[ing] upon a career of desolation" (116). He saw humans as particularly vulnerable to spores, "so like to animal cells," he writes, "as to have the power of penetrating into, and germinating upon, the most interior tissues of the human body" (136). Like Poe's fungi, Mitchell's were an alien and maleficent force operating nearly undetectably and distinguished by their "diffusion and number [...] their poisonous properties, and their peculiar seasons of growth, for the minuteness of their spores and for their love of darkness and tainted soils, and heavy atmospheres" (37).

Intensifying this nineteenth-century mycophobia was the speed at which micro-fungi could become macro-fungi. The ability of fungi to produce mushrooms depends on a form of growth radically different from human cell division: existing cells fill with water over a matter of hours during fruiting, sometimes with enough force to break and lift pavement. In the nineteenth century, however, this scale-shifting was regarded as a particularly inexplicable feature of fungal growth. Emily Dickinson's (1874) late poem "The Mushroom is the Elf of Plants—" offers a rare example of admiring ambivalence towards this rapid shift. As such, it is an interesting precursor of twentieth-century shifts in attitude towards fungi. Dickinson's poem locates fungal rebellion against human ideas about "Nature" in the incredible speed of fungal growth from invisible micro-matter to undeniable macro-matter.

In comparisons that leap and bound, Dickinson compares the mushroom to a "Truffled Hut," a "Juggler," a "Germ," and an "Apostate," evoking both whimsical delight and a faint whiff of menace. These quick shifts in the metaphorical vehicle for the mushroom seem to echo, or perhaps even parody, the multitude of fungal forms. This appears to be what makes fungi an apostasy within the natural world — that they grow "unnaturally" fast, springing from apparent nothingness to "Truffled Hut" overnight. They trouble the slow, deliberate, and apparent order of organismal cell division in apparent renunciation of Nature's laws. Literally and figuratively sporadic, the mushroom appears and disappears in ways that are at odds with the limits of human perception and expectation.

But the poem's comparisons also point out that fungi, in their uncannily invisible growth, are always present, even when they are not perceived by humans. While the vehicle of each metaphor shifts and twists and turns, the tenor, the mushroom itself, remains stable and insistent. Fungus does not take a single, scalable shape, but it stays at least partially itself, thus resisting human expectations that the nonhuman world will behave in an ordered, determinate, or visible way.

Dickinson's mushroom is also unusual in offering an alternative social order, replacing hierarchy with kinship. The elf and solo juggler of the first few stanzas give way to a scene of strange and contingent interconnection and interrelation by the end of the poem. The grass seems oddly "pleased" to have the mushroom "intermit," and the speaker determines that the mushroom is a "scion," or son, of "Summer's circumspect." The secret child of a season growing in every direction and at every scale, the mushroom is linked by kinship to those nonhuman forces of warmth and humidity that catalyze it. The multispecies collaborations for which fungi are known scientifically — from lichen to digestion to breaking down other dead organisms — seem to resonate with a fungus whose "smallness here," as Angela Sorby puts it, "invites the formation of interdependent, interspecies bonds" (2017, 314) as well as associations with the large-scale forces of the season. These are not necessarily always harmonious relationships in Dickinson's poem, but they are instances of connection and interrelation.

If Dickinson found in fungus an emblem of both multispecies and broadly nonhuman interconnection, much of British and American literature that came after tended to regard fungal scale-shifting more narrowly as a byword for uncanny degenerative growth. Some scientific accounts into the twentieth century continued to suggest that fungi had devolved from algae into parasitic plants, and there was ongoing confusion as to whether fungal cells were plant or animal. Canonical modernist literature consistently linked fungus and cultural "degeneracy" as well. Fungus appears in Ernest Hemingway's (1925) "Big Two-Hearted River" as a human-spread scourge of the natural world, and in Ezra Pound's cantos "fungus" is used as an insult and slur. D.H. Lawrence uses fungi's "smooth" exterior and "wormy" interior to excoriate the male bourgeoisie as "sickening toadstools" that would be best kicked over to "melt back, swiftly / into the soil of England" (1993, 430–31). As Anthony Camara (2014, n.p.) points out, fungi were a "preferred natural-supernatural menace among practitioners of Weird fiction." Science fiction by H.G. Wells (2000) was full of lively, if also menacing, fungi, featuring lunar fungal jungles and a psychoactive purple pileus. Later in the century, H.P. Lovecraft (2013) followed suit with fungoid aliens and fungal infestations, as well as a fungal sonnet cycle. Fungi, for these writers of Weird Fiction, were disruptive, unfamiliar forms of being so pervasive, invisible, and inevitable that they became a descriptor for the whole genre, and acclaimed writer of speculative fiction China Miéville recently described Weird Fiction in general as growing "like mould, mildew-damp, eldritch, its vectors vermiform" (2012, 1116).

Feminist writers, however, have regarded the growth of fungi from micro to macro with a more positive mix of suspicion and interest as a model for social disruption. The tradition stretches from the fungal growth in Charlotte Perkins Gilman's (1892) *The Yellow Wall Paper,* which Agnes Malinowska (2019) has linked to a threatening ideal of rapid and uncontrollable female reproduction, to Sylvia Plath's poem "Mushrooms" from 1960. For Plath, mushrooms figure a powerful underground rebellion akin to that of mid-century white, bourgeois femininity, rising "very / Whitely, very quietly [...] asking // Little or nothing" (2018, 139). The mid-century nuclear mushroom cloud, which, as Spencer Weart points out, was commonly used as a sign of the abrupt, large-scale transmutation of energy, provides a help-ful contrast: Plath's mushrooms are both diffident and relent-less, meek figures that will, nevertheless, "[i]nherit the earth" (2012, 140).

This interest in the surreptitious force of fungi presages the shift from a predominantly white, male response to fungi to the more diverse art and literature of the late twentieth and twenty-first centuries, which orients itself around the very disruptions that rendered fungi suspect to earlier writers. While the focus is still on macro-fungi for most writers, the ecological role of fun-gi as saprophytes, or decomposers, and their operation at differ-ent scales becomes much more central. Representative of this change is Pattiann Rogers's celebratory description of fungal elements of compost in the poem "Geocentric," which describes the many forms of fungal life in a compost pile as constitut-ing "the warm seethe of inevitable / putrefaction" (in Roehl and Chadwick 2010, 72). *Decomposition,* a 2010 anthology of fungi-inspired poems, demonstrates a view broadly held by these di-verse poets that fungi are the ugly but useful underdogs of the natural world. Yusef Komunyakaa's "Slime Molds" exemplifies this view: he describes slime molds as "good / For nothing" to being "good for something we never thought / about" (2000, 11). Fungi are likewise celebrated as symbols of the continuity of life through their association with the erotic in poems such as Alberto Ríos's "Prayer for the Dangerous" (in Roehl and Chadwick 2010, 38). Further, fungal interest moves steadily towards the invisible, the mycelial, and the spiritual. As poet Arthur Sze puts it, "I know in this meadow my passions are mycorrhizal with nature" (2021, 67).

This twenty-first century turn towards micro-mycophilia is even more explicitly articulated in mycology. The contemporary study of fungi has come to integrate technology and philosophy, with an emphasis on the invisible and microscopic forces of hyphae and mycelia rather than on mushrooms. Further, as mycologist and popular science writer Merlin Sheldrake points out, the field has shifted to understanding fungi as "inventive, flexible, and collaborative" organisms that are "veteran survivors of ecological catastrophe" (2020, 176). As scientists have gained interest in mycorrhizal networks as players in the "wood wide web," a parallel public interest in what Sheldrake calls "DIY mycology" has developed (2020, 122). Mycologist Paul Stamets's work on "mycoremediation," or the use of fungi to remedy ecological issues and health problems caused by humans, is central to this movement. Straddling professional and citizen science, alternative medicine, and entrepreneurship, Stamets's (2005) *Mycelium Running* articulates a myco-utopianism that finds in mycelia a source of sustainable building materials, a tool for toxic cleanups, and the route to mental and physical human health. Further, fungi here serve as a model for resisting and healing the intellectual and psychological wounds induced by Western individualism. Peter McCoy's (2016) *Radical Mycology* builds on this work by emphasizing mycological pedagogies, and he also co-hosts an influential "Radical Mycology Convergence" each year for the purpose of building "a mycelial network of like-minded fungi advocates" who will move humans "from domination toward allyship with the Fungal Queendom" ("About the RMC").

This mix of environmental, social, spiritual, personal, and entrepreneurial goals alternatively treats fungi as a flexible new tool to "improve the health of our lives and landscapes" and represents fungi as an honored and powerful subject in its own right. Mainstream accounts of fungal potential — such as science writer Michael Pollan's (2019) *How to Change Your Mind* and Sheldrake's (2020) *Entangled Life: How Fungi Make Our Worlds, Change Our Minds, and Shape Our Futures* — have popularized these reconsiderations of fungi's micro-to-macro capabilities as a utopian model and a potent material resource.

On a sometimes intertwining track, cultural theory has also arrived at a mycophilic, and microphilic, take on fungi. Rather than coordinating individual empowerment with environmental and social good, this literature primarily prizes fungal interdependence as a model for collective resistance to social, political, and economic hegemonies. The rhizome as a metaphor for disruptive social interrelation was articulated early on by Gilles Deleuze and Félix Guattari (1987) in *A Thousand Plateaus,* which resisted "arborescent," or vertical, interrelations in favor of the more lateral, interlinking "rhizome." As Patricia de Vries (2018) points out, this shift, while not explicitly fungal, nevertheless set the stage for the celebration of symbiotic or mutualistic relationships between plants and fungi. It is Anna Lowenhaupt Tsing (2015), however, who explicitly links "species interdependence" with fungal forms in her anthropological and philosophical account of matsutake foraging, *The Mushroom at the End of the World: On the Possibility of Life in Capitalist Ruins.* Tsing's influential project is explicitly attuned to questions of environmental justice and material precariousness. She explores the "overgrown verges of our blasted landscapes — the edges of capitalist discipline, scalability, and abandoned resource plantations" (282) through mushrooms because of their interdependence on other organisms, including the human. As she says: "No 'one' fungal body lives self-contained, removed from indeterminate encounters" (239). Further, Tsing uses these indeterminate, interdependent, and often invisible fungal morphologies to model newly contingent modes of thinking, in which we might "speculate about open-ended questions […] in a spore-like way" (239).

The entanglements of environmentalism, biotechnology, public health, and social marginalization in the critical discourse about fungus have made its ability to move quickly from micro to macro an attractive medium, and subject, for visual, conceptual, and design artists. The uses of micro-fungi in the arts range widely, from inoculating books with spores and presenting the be-mushroomed volumes as "translations," as artist Stephen Emmerson does, to major fungi-focused exhibitions in London and Berlin, in which artists and designers use inoculated objects to construct everything from Theresa Schubert's (2020) sonicated hyphae to Kristel Peters's fungal shoe to Jae Rhim Lee's (2011) fungal burial suit. Peters's shoe and Lee's suit address the leather and funeral industries, respectively, in that they purportedly train fungi to replace toxic processes. Viewers of Schubert's work can engage in a kind of conversation with fungus by altering mycelial growth through sound, and this project likewise allows viewers to "fluidly shift from a macro view to a cellular level" within fungal networks ("Sound for Fungi"). Micro-fungi appear here to counter Western individualism and greed in both material and conceptual forms as a quick-growing remedial biotechnology, a conceptual model for mutualistic networks, and a conversing subject. In contrast to Alice's distressed puzzlement at fungi's relentless, uncanny shapeshifting, or Dickinson's ambivalent admiration for the fungal rebel, contemporary poet and essayist Ross Gay (2019) wholeheartedly embraces microscopic fungal networks in his *Book of Delights*: "the trees and the mushrooms," he says,

> have shown me this — joy is the mostly invisible, the underground union between us, you and me, which is, among other things, the great fact of our life and the lives of everyone and thing we love going away. If we sink a spoon into that fact, into the duff between us, we will find it teeming. It will look like all the books ever written. It will look like all the nerves in a body. We might call it sorrow, but we might call

it a union, one that, once we notice it, once we bring it into the light, might become flower and food. Might be joy. (163)

Gay's fungal aesthetic is of our moment: for us, micro-fungi are both invisible and essential, vulnerable and resistant, at once a sign and an incarnation of our promising and perilous interdependency on what we cannot see.

References and Further Reading

"About the RMC." n.d. *Radical Mycology Convergence*. https:// radicalmycologyconvergence.com/pages/about-the-rmc-1.

Altschuler, Sari. 2018. *The Medical Imagination: Literature and Health in the Early United States*. Philadelphia: University of Pennsylvania Press.

Bertelsen, Cynthia D. 2013. *Mushroom: A Global History*. London: Reaktion Books.

Bone, Eugenia. 2013. *Mycophilia: Revelations from the Weird World of Mushrooms*. Emmaus: Rodale.

Camara, Anthony. 2014. "Abominable Transformations: Becoming-Fungus in Arthur Machen's *The Hill of Dreams*." *Gothic Studies* 16, no. 1: 9–23. DOI: 10.7227/gs.16.1.2.

Carroll, Lewis. 1865. *Alice's Adventures in Wonderland*. Illustrated by John Tenniel. London: Macmillan and Co.

Chesnutt, Charles W., and R.J. Ellis. 2014. *The Colonel's Dream*. Morgantown: West Virginia University Press.

Cojak, Kristel. n.d. "Kristel Peters: Growing Shoes with Mycelium." *Mediamatic*. https://www.mediamatic.net/nl/ page/87776/kristel-peters.

Darwin, Erasmus. 2017. *The Botanic Garden, Part II*. Edited by Adam Komisaruk and Allison Dushane. London: Routledge.

Deleuze, Gilles, and Félix Guattari. 1987. *A Thousand Plateaus: Capitalism and Schizophrenia*. Translated by Brian Massumi. London: Bloomsbury.

de Vries, Patricia. 2018. "When Fungus Punched Anthropos in the Gut: On Crap, Fish-Eating Trees, Rhizomes and Organized Networks." *Rhizomes: Cultural Studies in Emerging Knowledge* 34. http://rhizomes.net/issue34/ devries.html. DOI: 10.20415/rhiz/034.e04.

Dickinson, Emily. "The Mushroom Is the Elf of Plants." Amherst College Digital Collections of the Amherst College Archives & Special Collections, Amherst Manuscript #417. https://acdc.amherst.edu/view/asc:13184/asc:13187.

Emmerson, Stephen. 2015. "Rilke Translations." *Stephen Emmerson,* October 28. https://stephenemmerson. wordpress.com/rilke-translations/.

Gay, Ross. 2019. *The Book of Delights: Essays.* Chapel Hill: Algonquin Books.

Gilman, Charlotte Perkins. 1892. *The Yellow Wall Paper.* Boston: Small, Maynard and Co.

Haraway, Donna. 2008. *When Species Meet.* Minneapolis: University of Minnesota Press.

Hemingway, Ernest. 1995. *The Collected Stories.* Edited by James Fenton. London: Everyman's Library.

Komunyakaa, Yusef. 2000. *Talking Dirty to the Gods.* New York: Farrar, Straus and Giroux.

Lawrence, D.H. 1993. *The Complete Poems of D.H. Lawrence.* Edited by Vivian De and Warren Roberts. New York: Penguin Books.

Lee, Jae Rhim. 2011. "My Mushroom Burial Suit." *Ted.* https:// www.ted.com/talks/jae_rhim_lee_my_mushroom_burial_ suit.

Lloyd, John Uri. 1895. *Etidorhpa; or, The End of Earth, the Strange History of a Mysterious Being and the Account of a Remarkable Journey as Communicated in Manuscript to Llewellyn Drury Who Promised to Print the Same, but Finally Evaded the Responsibility Which Was Assumed.* Cincinnati: J.U. Lloyd.

Lovecraft, H.P. 2013. *Fungi from Yuggoth.* Illustrated by D.M. Mitchell. Washington, DC: Apophenia Press.

———. 2017. *The Complete Fiction.* Oxford: Benediction Classics.

Malinowska, Agnes. 2019. "Charlotte Perkins Gilman's Fungal Female Animal: Evolution, Efficiency, and the Reproductive Body." *Modernism/Modernity* 26, no. 2: 267–88. DOI: 10.1353/ mod.2019.0031.

McCoy, Peter. 2016. *Radical Mycology: A Treatise on Seeing and Working with Fungi.* Portland: Chthaeus Press.

Miéville, China. 2012. "Afterweird." In *The Weird: A Compendium of Strange and Dark Stories,* edited by Jeffrey VanderMeer and Ann VanderMeer, 1113–16. New York: Tor Books.

Millman, Lawrence, and Amy Jean Porter. 2019. *Fungipedia: A Brief Compendium of Mushroom Lore.* Princeton: Princeton University Press.

Mitchell, John Kearsley. 1859. *Five Essays.* Edited by Silas Weir Mitchell. Philadelphia: J.B. Lippincott & Co.

Money, Nicholas P. 2007. *The Triumph of the Fungi: A Rotten History.* Oxford: Oxford University Press.

Money, Nicholas P. 2011. *Mushroom.* Oxford: Oxford University Press.

———. 2018. *The Rise of Yeast: How the Sugar Fungus Shaped Civilization.* Oxford: Oxford University Press.

"Mykoweb." n.d. *Mykoweb.* http://www.mykoweb.eu/.

Plath, Sylvia. 2018. *The Collected Poems.* Edited by Ted Hughes. New York: Harper Perennial Modern Classics.

Pollan, Michael. 2019. *How To Change Your Mind: The New Science of Psychedelics.* London: Penguin Books.

Poe, Edgar Allan. 1845. *Tales by Edgar A. Poe.* New York: Wiley and Putnam.

Roehl, Renée, and Kelly Chadwick, eds. 2010 *Decomposition: An Anthology of Fungi-Inspired Poems.* Sandpoint: Lost Horse Press.

Rolfe, R.T., and F.W. Rolfe. 1974. *The Romance of the Fungus World: An Account of Fungus Life in Its Numerous Guises, Both Real and Legendary.* New York: Dover Editions.

Schubert, Theresa. 2020. "Sound for Fungi: Homage to Indeterminacy." *Theresa Schubert.* http://theresaschubert.com/artworks/art/sound-for-fungi-homage-to-indeterminacy/#images-videos.

Sheldrake, Merlin. 2020. *Entangled Life: How Fungi Make Our Worlds, Change Our Minds and Shape Our Futures.* London: The Bodley Head Ltd.

Sorby, Angela. 2017. "'A Dimple in the Tomb': Cuteness in Emily Dickinson." *ESQ: A Journal of Nineteenth-Century American Literature and Culture* 63, no. 2: 297–328. DOI: 10.1353/esq.2017.0011.

Stamets, Paul. 2005. *Mycelium Running: How Mushrooms Can Help Save the World.* Berkeley: Ten Speed Press.

Sze, Arthur. 2021. *The Glass Constellation: New and Collected Poems.* Port Townsend: Copper Canyon Press.

Tsing, Anna Lowenhaupt. 2017. *The Mushroom at the End of The World: On the Possibility of Life in Capitalist Ruins.* Princeton: Princeton University Press.

Verne, Jules. 2008. *Journey to the Centre of the Earth.* Translated by Robert Baldick. London: Puffin Classics.

Wasson, R. Gordon, and Valentina Pavlovna Wasson. 1957. *Mushrooms, Russia, and History.* New York: Pantheon Books.

Weart, Spencer R. 2012. *The Rise of Nuclear Fear.* Cambridge: Harvard University Press.

Wells, H.G. 2020. *The First Men in the Moon.* London: Arcturus Publishing.

———. 2000. *The Complete Short Stories.* Edited by John Hammond. London: Phoenix Press.

CHAPTER 5

Lichen

Helga G. Braunbeck

Contemplating the enigmatic shapes and configurations in which lichen grows on the ground, Woyzeck, the protagonist of nineteenth-century German writer Georg Büchner's stage play of the same name, wonders: "Who might be able to read this?" The ability to "read nature" has, along with the development of modern science and its tools, expanded knowledge in at least two new directions. As the microscope discovered increasingly smaller units of organic and inorganic matter and micromatter, the field of microbiology, and eventually genetics, were developed. Starting with scientist and explorer Alexander von Humboldt, this field gained a broader perspective on the complex interactions between organisms within local and regional ecosystems and their dynamic interrelations within the global biosphere, or possibly even space. Both of these expansions of human knowledge — peering into the microcosm of life and trying to grasp its place in the universe — have changed the narrative of natural history and the theory of evolution, including how organisms are classified and even the underlying concept of what constitutes an "individual" species or organism. Inspecting cells and identifying genes has made it possible to understand the evolution and functioning of many organisms better. This is particularly true for lichen, which had remained enigmatic for a long time and then turned out to be among the most ancient and long-living life-forms on earth. And engaging the global view made possible by satellites in space and other airborne objects "looking down" onto the blue-green planet has revealed this organism's impressive spatial extension. Lichen occupies about eight percent of earth's terrestrial surface and consists of likely more than 25,000 species.

In 1732, Swedish biologist Carl Linnaeus, who established the scientific system of plant taxonomy and nomenclature, traveled through Lapland, land of the Indigenous Sami reindeer herders of Northern Europe. In his travel diary, he identified numerous lichens. But it was Linnaeus's student, Erik Acharius, who so significantly expanded the classification of lichen species that he became known as the "father of lichenology." Much later, in the twentieth century, the collection and taxonomic classification of thousands of specimens from the southern hemisphere would be added to this knowledge base by the "unsung heroine of lichenology," Elke Mackenzie. The story of this species is quite intriguing. Despite some of its leafy or shrubby structures, lichen is actually not a plant. It was and still is classified as a fungus, which constitutes its main body, the "thallus." In 1869, Swiss botanist Simon Schwendener discovered that lichen consists of two or more organisms that maintain a symbiosis, that is, a mutually beneficial form of coexistence, in this case between a fungus and algae or cyanobacteria or, as was later discovered, sometimes all three. The word "symbiosis" was coined in 1877 by German botanist Albert Bernhard Frank specifically to describe the association of the partners that constitute lichen. Even today, the nature of this symbiotic relationship is not yet fully understood, as biologist Merlin Sheldrake confirms when he calls lichens "living riddles" (2020, 71).

Over time, scientists and science writers have employed metaphors borrowed from human social relationships in order to capture this apparently unusual arrangement. Is this symbiotic organism, "nature's power couple," engaged in a romantic relationship or even a marriage? Or is it rather a parasitic "master-slave" relationship in which one partner holds the other one captive, an "exploiter" and its "victim"? When it was discovered that more than two could be involved, some asked whether it should be described as a "ménage à trois"? Or are lichens perhaps "'fungi who discovered agriculture' by capturing photo-synthetic beings," as Robin Wall Kimmerer states (2013, 271)? Is their relationship truly mutualistic and reciprocal? These meta-phors convey the struggle of scientists to understand a living arrangement that seemed so unusual in the world of vegetal be-ings that it prompted them to look for relational patterns from the human world. Their metaphors also reflect the cultures and worldviews of their historical periods as well as the status of scientific knowledge at the time.

Entering into a collaboration to survive in extreme, climati-cally and nutritionally challenging environments, eventually the lichen way of life turned out to be not so strange after all. Mi-crobiologist and evolutionary theorist Lynn Margulis rewrote the history of life with her theory that symbiosis, the "living-together" of two or more species, even from separate kingdoms, was actually a key driver of evolution and that this "interliv-ing — symbiogenesis — made habitation of the hostile, new dry land possible for life" (1998, 107). Due to its role in rock weath-ering, the pioneer species lichen contributed to soil formation, thus preparing the ground for later species to develop. Fittingly, since lichen transforms inorganic matter into organic matter that supports life, Sheldrake calls lichens the "go-betweens that inhabit the boundary between life and nonlife" (2020, 75).

Lichen has become the poster child for symbiosis, and its life as a symbiotic partnership allows lichen to thrive in marginal habitats with little moisture and nutrition, extreme cold or heat, as well as in temperate regions and urban environments. It can even survive in outer space. The fungus (the "mycobiont") fur-nishes the lichen with a physical structure and protects its algal or cyanobacterial partner (the "photobiont") from excess light, while also providing it with moisture and minerals. The photo-biont, which resides inside the body of the fungus, in turn pro-duces nutrition. The fungus has no leaves and no chlorophyll,

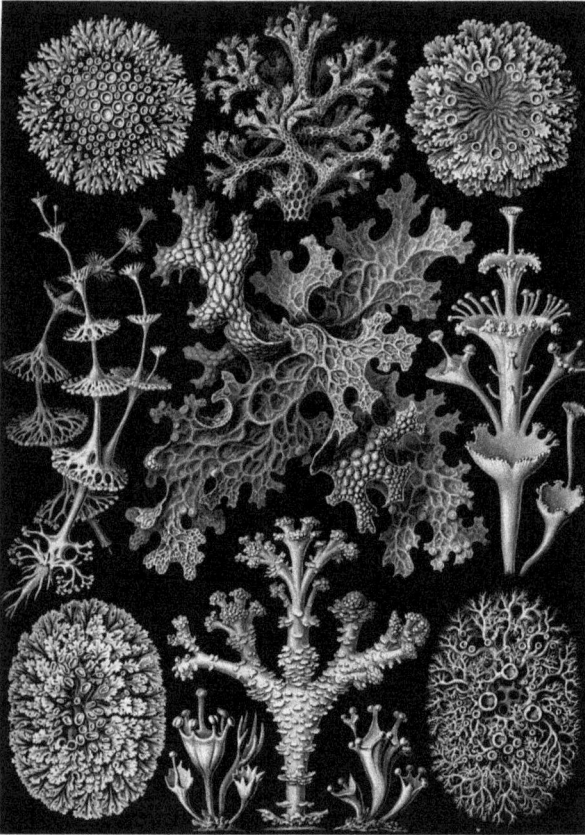

Fig. 1. German biologist Ernst Haeckel's 1904 black-and-white depiction of lichens highlights their forms.

so it is the photosynthesis of the algae or bacteria that produces sugars and other carbohydrates for all of them.

Lacking roots, lichen attaches itself with a stalk or its fungal filaments to a large variety of surfaces or substrates. It grows on rocks, bark, wood, leaves, mosses and dead matter, other lichens, soil, animals, and human-made surfaces such as concrete, metal, glass, or discarded objects, and even plastic. Lichen can actually penetrate a rock and grow inside of it, thereby decomposing it. Some "vagrant" species do not attach to any surface at all. The growth rate of lichen is extremely slow, often less than a millimeter per year. For lichens growing in a radial form, measurements from the center can be used to establish their age as well as the age of the substrate in a simple process called lichenometry. And lichens can grow very old. At more than 9,000 years old, an arctic lichen living in Swedish Lapland is among the oldest living organisms on earth (Sheldrake 2020, 85).

Since lichen has no flowers and consists of two or more organisms, its reproduction is complicated and takes on various forms. Its fungus may produce sexual fruiting bodies containing spores, which must land close to the right algae or cyanobacteria with which this particular species of fungus can enter into a lichen symbiosis. Such dependence on chance might not lead to reproductive success. Therefore, lichen can also reproduce asexually or vegetatively, by breaking off fragments that are then dispersed by wind, water, or animals. These clonal fragments already contain cells from all the partners needed for symbiosis, increasing the chances for successful reproduction.

Lichens display a tremendous diversity of forms and colors, and they may grow like mushrooms, have leafy or shrubby structures, form crusts, powders, jellies, stringy, hairy, or wispy structures hanging from trees, or have little structure at all. German biologist Ernst Haeckel's 1904 black and white depiction of lichens highlights some of these forms (see fig. 1). And Tomas Castelazo's photograph displays the brilliant colors of a lichen community composed of various species (see fig. 2). Lichen color is usually determined by their photobiont and changes depending on the habitat and how wet or dry they are. When wet, they shine in brilliant yellow, orange, or red. And in the dry, desiccated state, which allows them to survive long droughts, colors will be more muted, gray or brown. But dried lichen keeps its shape, which is why it can simulate trees and shrubbery in architectural and model train landscapes. In nature, lichen paints the landscape, especially in regions devoid of other vegetation, an aesthetic value prized by photographers. One of its main uses

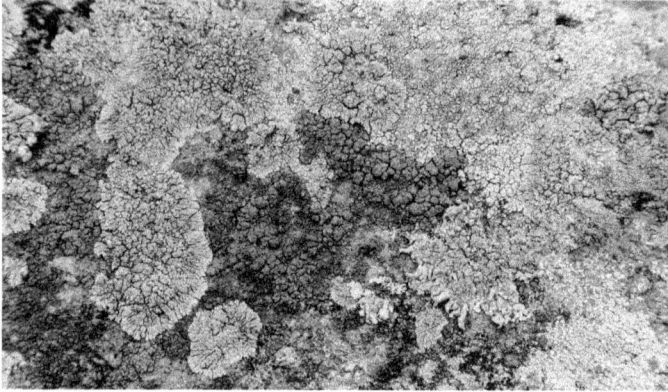

Fig. 2. Tomas Castelazo's photograph of "various species of lychen covering a rock" displays the brilliant colors of lichen. CC BY-SA 4.0.

by humans is making natural dyes, as in Navajo blankets and Scottish tartans.

Indigenous peoples also turn to lichen as a food source in times of emergency and extract its fibers to make clothing. Even the biblical manna — the food provided to the Israelites by God while they were traveling through the desert after their exodus from Egypt — is thought to have been lichen. With its antibiotic properties, as well as its use in the treatment of respiratory infections, lichen also has medicinal value. Only one species, "wolf lichen," is poisonous.

Birds and squirrels depend on lichen for nesting material, and herbivores for food, especially caribou in North America and reindeer in Europe, and their winter diet consists of 90 percent lichen. The advancing climate crisis threatens lichen, and as a result, Indigenous Sami cultures dependent on reindeer herding are in a precarious position, as are wild reindeer herds. And in 1986, radiation from the Chernobyl nuclear accident contaminated lichen, necessitating the slaughter of many herds, as their milk and meat had become unfit for human consumption.

While lichen has the ability to survive droughts by entering into a dormant, desiccated state, it is highly sensitive to pollution. It is therefore used to monitor air quality, serving, for instance, as a bioindicator of the presence of sulfur dioxide released in the burning of fossil fuels. Human impact on lichen is primarily negative, and we threaten lichen's survival through air pollution, habitat devastation, and rising temperatures resulting from the emission of greenhouse gasses. Considering lichen's amazing qualities and usefulness to human and more-than-human creatures alike, it is not surprising that this organism has garnered attention beyond its ecological significance, becoming the subject of reflection in a number of cultural contexts.

Literary Lichenology

Despite being neither tall like trees nor showy like flowers, lichen has attracted the fascination of literary writers in particular. They have explored its diversity of forms, symbiotic lifestyle, longevity, and persistent mystery in their poetry and prose. Lichen has been linguistically recreated and cultivated in many different yet connected ways, resulting in a network of literary lichens that reflects the diversity of its forms.

Three contemporary American poets interweave the motif of lichen's inconspicuousness and remaining mystery with scientific facts about its symbiotic lifestyle and ecosystem services, applying an earth-historical perspective. Lew Welch starts his poem "Springtime in the Rockies, Lichen" (2012) with the statement: "All these years I overlooked them" (145), and in her poem "For the Lobaria, Usnea, Witches Hair, Map Lichen, Beard Lichen, Ground Lichen, Shield Lichen," Jane Hirshfield admits: "Back then, what did I know?" (2011, 34). After these initial statements, both poets incorporate scientific knowledge about their newfound object of interest, such as when Welch calls the organism a "symbiotic splash of plant and fungus" (145), and Hirshfield turns to the relationship metaphor of a "marriage of fungi and algae" (34). Both comment on lichen's ability to dissolve rock, Welch by calling it a "crumbler-of-the-rocks" (2012, 146), and Hirshfield by referring to lichens as "transformers unvalued" (2011, 34), thus alluding to lichen's function as a creator of the soil that allows plants to grow and other life to develop. Both poets wonder about lichen's exchanges with its environment, and Hirshfield admires how lichens can take nutrients from the air, making them "chemists of the air" (34) while Welch asks, "How can the poisons reach them?" (2012, 146), likely referring to lichen's sensitivity to air pollution. They also include their personal observations of this "grey-green, incomprehensible, old" organism (Hirshfield 2011, 34). Even a magnifying glass fails to penetrate lichen's secrets, as Welch contemplates, "where do the plants begin? Why are they doing this?" and finally "why am I made to kneel and peer at Tiny?" (2012, 145). In his title poem of the 2021 collection of the same name, "Twice Alive," Forrest Gander also focuses on lichen's biological properties, but uses more scientific terminology, such as "mycobiont," "umbilicate lichens," or "cordyceps" (2021, 17, 20). He complements his observations through a magnifying glass with sensory impressions, such as the smell of lichen's fragrance. Current scientific research, which is deciphering ever more of this mysterious organism's codes and secrets, such as its crucial role for the development of life on earth and its important function as an indicator species for pollution and climate change, can certainly offer guidance for an environmentally aware person for how to establish a relationship with this stranger and take inspiration from it for poetic creativity.

Admiration for lichen's ability to overcome modern society's nature-culture divide and live within a completely hostile urban environment drives the impetus for German writer Marion Poschmann's "Ode an die Bordsteinflechte" ("Ode to the Sidewalk Lichen") (2020, 69–70, my translation). Employing the same gesture of kneeling that Welch had mentioned, the poet has her speaker marvel at lichen growing on old granite plates in front of the entrance to a laundromat and a dog-grooming business. Living among accumulated detritus like chewing gum, it is constantly trodden on by humans and dogs. The speaker's attempt to capture the lichen with tracing paper, an exercise in "willow leaf gray" that displays a "secret zen garden," reveals what looks like the internal structure of the stone, a pattern the lichen has produced by growing into the stone. She questions what this "wilderness" might be hiding from her, and why she is even seeking answers from this "stain" of lichen. The organism's ability to preserve and bring its wilderness into the realm of human urban culture is beyond her comprehension and her own capacity for forming a deep, meaningful connection.

While Poschmann and Welch struggle to arrive at a better understanding of this strange organism, American poet Arthur Sze chooses to give his literary lichen agency and let it speak, confronting and accusing humans of their failure to nurture a caring relationship with their nonhuman, earthly co-inhabitants. Sze's "Lichen Song" (2016) is a narrative poem told from the perspective of lichen growing in his house "on the ceiling wood" above the shower stall. The lichen confronts humans with the charge of neglect, claiming "you don't care," and "you don't understand." It explains its characteristics, such as respiring instead of breathing, its slow growth, and its ability to survive extreme cold temperatures and even the "cosmic rays" of space. The speaking lichen develops hypotheses — "if you slowed you could discover" — but ends with the accusation that humans really only pay attention to lichens now because they are "about to leave," a reference to posthuman times, in which lichen, but not humans, will presumably continue to exist.

What has led to this state of alienation between humans and lichen? Sami poet Nils-Aslak Valkeapää has an answer. The colonization of Indigenous lands, which destroyed ancient ways of life, is to blame, along with the machines and pollution of industrial modernity, in which the planetary impact ushered in a new geological epoch, the Anthropocene. In his poetry collection, *Trekways of the Wind* (an anthology of poems written between 1974 and 1981), he uses a satirical and accusatory tone to portray the colonization of ancestral lands by "Homo Sapiens the wise human" and the ensuing devastation of grazing lands, the pollution of rivers, and the wounding of the earth by "ugly machines" (1994, n.p.). He asks, "what is it that makes the reindeer die when they graze on scanty lands' crumbled and poisoned lichen?" (1994, n.p.). The devastation of nature by human "civilization" seems to have no limits, affecting even remote areas, destroying ancient cultures, and killing the living beings that are the basis for their animal and human lives: lichen. Both Sze and Valkeapää demonstrate the interconnectedness of the human and nonhuman worlds, and they articulate how disregard for other-than-human beings ultimately leads to the demise of humankind. While he addressed environmental degradation affecting lichen and Indigenous cultures in his earlier poetry collection, *The Sun, My Father* (1988), Valkeapää articulates a kind of communication between lichen and the poet, one that features speaking lichen as in Sze's poem. He gives agency to this nonhuman Other when he writes how "the lichen on the pebbles, the reindeer moss / opens itself / moves / comes alive" (n.p.), and, along with the wind, whispers and speaks to him and creates his song. Since Sami poetry is first and foremost part of an oral culture, in which poetry is presented as a song called the "yoik," the lichen in Valkeapää's poem "whispers and speaks" as it "makes a yoik" (n.p.). It thus asserts its agency, poetic creativity, and ability to bridge the artificial nature-culture divide of Western modernity, which is responsible for the devastation of Indigenous, sustainable ways of living in harmony with nature.

While lichen participates in the oral Sami culture by whispering, speaking, and singing, German post-war poet Hans Magnus Enzensberger imagines his literary lichen as a participant in Western civilization's written knowledge tradition, presenting a comprehensive lexicon of lichen in his poem of twenty stanzas, "Flechtenkunde" ("Lichenology"), originally from 1964 (2009, my translation). The poet investigates all aspects of lichen, its scientific properties, service to humans and ecosystems, and role in earth's history, and he even notices similarities between its symbiotic lifestyle and a human economic system. In an essay published much later, in 2009, which includes the poem, the poet explains that he is fascinated by the mystery surrounding lichen. Accordingly, as did Hirshfield and Poschmann, he asks many questions in the poem. And as did his predecessor Büchner, whom he quotes, Enzensberger focuses on the visual, script-like shapes that lichen produces on the ground. While Büchner has his Woyzeck-figure wondering about how to "read" the messages that lichen seems to inscribe on the ground, Enzensberger, using a different perspective, gives agency to lichen and allegorizes it as a species that, like literary authors, writes. However, its original script is written in code, and lichen "describes itself, inscribes itself, writes, in encoded script, a verbose silence: *Graphis scripta*" (2009, 831). The only lichen species mentioned in his poem by its scientific name, the "script lichen" or "secret writing lichen," entices the poet to decipher its code, investigate its genus, and capture its characteristics and history in metaphors and allegory (2009, 831). He explores the organism's unique temporality, calling it "earth's slowest telegram" and, due to its longevity and ability to "write," considers it earth's "big memory" (2009, 831, 834). He honors lichen symbiosis for the collectivization of its production, valuing its collaborative communism over competitive capitalism and its nondestructive relation to other species and nonorganic objects as pacifism. Reversing the established view of evolution, humans are, in the speaker's view, "not yet" this far advanced (2009, 834). In an interview about his poem, Enzensberger calls symbiosis the greatest invention of biology, admires lichen's intelligence, and considers our present-day digital networking as originating in the evolution of lichen.

While the life of micro-matter such as lichen may attract more attention from writers employing literature's small form, the poem, it nonetheless contains plenty of intriguing material for larger forms, such as the novel. John Wyndham's 1960 science fiction narrative *Trouble with Lichen,* for instance, explores how the commercial and political exploitation of a rare lichen's supposed anti-aging properties tests the consciences of two scientists. Like Enzensberger, Wyndham establishes a connection between lichen and political economy, only his is not based on lichen's symbiotic way of life but on its longevity, which can now, through injections of the extract "lichenin," be transferred to humans. Wyndham explores how extending human life would completely upset the current political-economic and social order, especially since lichenin would not be widely available for the specific lichen species only grows, very slowly, in small colonies in "northern Manchuria, close to the Russian border" (1960, 179). So, Wyndham has his protagonist, a female scientist, leave her research position and pursue a beauty business, in which only women secretly receive this "antigerone" that will stop the aging process. This female-only life extension presents an opportunity to overturn entrenched patriarchal power structures and realize a long overdue feminist revolution. There is a certain irony in the fact that one of earth's longest-living organisms would be monetized in a capitalist system and used to overthrow one of human civilization's longest-enduring power structures. Or maybe this sci-fi novel suggests that the stereotypical association of women and "nature" could actually be weaponized within the male-dominated capitalist system in order to change it from within and establish a female-dominated society through the power of "nature," a kind of female human-nature symbiosis.

Symbiosis is also the central theme in Swiss author Barbara Schibli's novel *Flechten* (*Lichens*) (2017, my translation), in which she weaves together lichen's complex way of life as a "double being" with the complicated relationship of identical twins, Anna and Leta. Narrator Anna is a lichen researcher, and this allows the author to discuss scientific findings about various lichen species and their ecologies as well as the social dynamics of the lichen research community. Anna's sister Leta is a photographer, who obsessively only photographs Anna, then exhibits the photographs in a show called "Observing the Self," thus erasing the boundary between them. In the sisters' co-dependent relationship, Leta is the dominant partner, who figuratively incorporates her sister's identity. This mirrors the relationship between the fungus and its photobiont. Like the fungus, which provides the external structure for the symbiosis, Leta dictates the terms of their association. And like the photobiont, which provides nutrition for the fungus, the photographs of Anna that Leta publicly exhibits, sustain her identity-stealing sister. Lichen's unique symbiotic properties fuel the extended metaphor for

Anna's attempts to disentangle herself from her identical twin who does not respect their relationship as a collaboration based on mutualism and reciprocity.

Just as the poems, the two novels highlight the complex interrelations that lichen presents and with which humans struggle, some on a more personal level and others at a larger scale, with lichen as the secret tool for reforming social structures. While science has illuminated many of lichen's characteristics and ways of life, literature is able to connect them with both the deep time of earth history and the history of humanity. Modeling a different way of relating and alerting humans about the impending environmental catastrophe, lichen also communicate through literary texts, addressing the future of all life on earth from the distant past.

Shifting Shapes and Paradigms

While Büchner's character Woyzeck marveled at lichen's mysterious and undecipherable messages, late twentieth- and early twenty-first literary writers were, with the help of science, able to "read" them and perceive lichen's agentive role as a writer and re-writer of evolutionary and human history. Joining scientists in their growing interest in symbiosis, they explored this form of life, engaging the lichen motif as a metaphor for a collaborative way of life, that may, despite its concomitant dangers, offer an alternative path forward for a humanity facing the risks and threats of the Anthropocene, or, as John Charles Ryan phrases it, "Licheness directs us toward greater harmonization with the Earth" (2021, n.p.). In the interest of a livable future for the global community, it would be prudent to rethink how humans could transform the current regime of exploitation to one that makes nature an equal partner in a system of co-living.

The partners of a lichen symbiosis mutually change each other while engaging in their collaborative way of life, which leads Gander in his poem "Twice Alive" to pose the question whether "all identity" may perhaps be "combinatory" (2021, 9). In the sciences, lichens are still classified only by their fungal partner, but since Margulis's discoveries, a paradigm shift has been underway, not by changing nomenclature, but by increasingly recognizing the significance of symbiosis for the evolution of life on earth. Instead of conceptualizing evolution on the basis of competition (the metaphor of the "survival of the fittest," based on Darwin's theories) and representing it as the tree of life (with only vertical gene transfer), scientists are now finding more and more evidence of collaboration between species through horizontal relationships, such as lichen symbiosis. Another horizontal collaboration, recently discovered by forest ecologist Suzanne Simard, are underground mycorrhizal forest networks of tree roots and fungi. And the possibility of horizontal gene transfer, that is, gene transfer not from parent to offspring (most common in bacteria, but also between other species), presents further support for this reconceptualization (see Sheldrake 2020, 77–78). Regarding lichens, which made networking their way of life early on in evolution, biologist David George Haskell acknowledges that this shift towards collaboration was worth it: "By stripping off the bonds of individuality the lichens have produced a world-conquering union" (2012, 3). As science is unraveling more and more of the mysteries of lichen and many other forms of life, it is also reconceptualizing how the evolution of life should be represented, not as a vertical tree of life but as a network with symbiotic relations reaching in many directions.

When French philosopher Jean-Luc Nancy (2000) claims in *Being Singular Plural* that there is no being without "being-with," that "I" does not precede "we," that all existence is coexistence and community, he might as well be describing symbiosis. New discoveries about communication between plants and fungi confirm the idea that biological networks "are symbiotic rather than competitive, based on shared interests rather than mutually exclusive gains," as plant philosopher Michael Marder puts it (2016, 95). The study of "nature" has moved from focusing on and classifying single organisms to considering environments and their ecological entanglements, the complete web of life. As an organism with a million-year history, lichen has known all along that collaboration is the ticket to survival, the only way forward in a world that is becoming increasingly hostile to life. Conceiving of life as symbiosis rather than competition, domination, and devastation, and finding new metaphors for the relations between living beings — intersections, mesh-like or rhizomatic networks, entanglements, webs — as Andreas Hejnol calls for in *Arts of Living on a Damaged Planet* (Tsing et al. 2017, G100). These are suggestions that deserve attention. Lichen already has the script for the future. Humans can now look to a marginalized yet truly marvelous little being not just as a mystery, but as a possible model for how to live, particularly in a world whose living conditions are becoming ever more extreme. After all, as Sheldrake puts it: "Lichens are small biospheres that include both photosynthetic and non-photosynthetic organisms, thus combining the earth's main metabolic processes. Lichens are in some sense micro-planets — worlds writ small" (2020, 83).

References and Further Reading

Brodo, Irwin M., Sylvia Duran Sharnoff, and Stephen Sharnoff. 2001. *Lichens of North America.* New Haven: Yale University Press.

Enzensberger, Hans Magnus. 2009. "Einiges über Flechten." In *Scharmützel und Scholien: Über Literatur,* 826–34. Frankfurt: Suhrkamp.

Gander, Forrest. 2021. *Twice Alive.* New York: New Directions.

Haskell, David George. 2012. *The Forest Unseen: A Year's Watch in Nature.* New York: Penguin Books.

Hirshfield, Jane. 2011. *Come, Thief.* New York: Knopf.

Kimmerer, Robin Wall. 2013. *Braiding Sweetgrass.* Minneapolis: Milkweed Editions.

Marder, Michael. 2016. *Grafts: Writings on Plants.* Minneapolis: University of Minnesota Press.

Margulis, Lynn. 1998. *Symbiotic Planet: A New Look at Evolution.* Amherst: Basic Books.

Nancy, Jean-Luc. 2000. *Being Singular Plural.* Translated by Robert Richardson and Anne O'Byrne. Stanford: Stanford University Press.

Poschmann, Marion. 2020. *Nimbus: Gedichte.* Berlin: Suhrkamp.

Purvis, William. 2000. *Lichens.* Washington, DC: Smithsonian Institution Press.

Rogers, Robert. 2011. *The Fungal Pharmacy: The Complete Guide to Medicinal Mushrooms and Lichens of North America.* Berkeley: North Atlantic Books.

Ryan, John Charles. 2021. "On Becoming Lichen." *Europe Now Journal,* November 9, 2021. https://www.europenowjournal. org/2021/11/07/on-becoming-lichen/.

Sheldrake, Merlin. 2020. *Entangled Life: How Fungi Make Our Worlds, Change Our Minds and Shape Our Futures.* New York: Random House.

Schibli, Barbara. 2017. *Flechten.* Zürich: Dörlemann.

Sze, Arthur. 2016. "Lichen Song." *Narrative Magazine.*
    https://www.narrativemagazine.com/issues/poems-
    week-2015-2016/poem-week/lichen-song-arthur-sze.
Tsing, Anna, Heather Swanson, Elaine Gan, and Nils Bubandt,
    eds. 2017. *Arts of Living on a Damaged Planet: Monsters of
    the Anthropocene.* Minneapolis: University of Minnesota
    Press.
Valkeapää, Nils-Aslak. 1988. *The Sun, My Father.*
    Guovdageaidnu: DAT.
———. 1994. *Trekways of the Wind.* Guovdageaidnu: DAT.
Welch, Lew. 2012. *Ring of Bone: Collected Poems.* San Francisco:
    City Lights Books.
Wyndham, John. 1960. *Trouble with Lichen.* London: Ballantine
    Books.

CHAPTER 6

Pollen

Joela Jacobs

When inhaling pollen, your body is penetrated by a little package of plant sperm. Pollen grains are multicellular organisms that contain male sex cells, and their job is to get this sperm to the egg to facilitate fertilization. Just like with humans, the sexual reproduction of seed plants and algae depends on the union of male and female sex cells, that is, sperm and egg. A traveler by design, pollen's origin and intended destination are plant genitals: the flowers of flowering plants and the cones of coniferous ones. Surrounded by a sturdy shell of sporopollenin to protect the sperm, the goal of a pollen grain is to move from a flower's male reproductive organ (stamen) to a female one (pistil), or from the male to the female cone. Flowers can have male, female, or both reproductive organs, depending on the kind of plant. In the case of self-pollinating plants that feature both, the pollen journey might be as short as from stamen to pistil in the same flower. Pollen grains that need to reach a neighboring flower, cone, or different plant hitch a ride on insects or trust their fate to wind, water, and any other moving means. Those with larger distances to cross have typically evolved one of a variety of mechanisms to optimize their chances at mobility: some

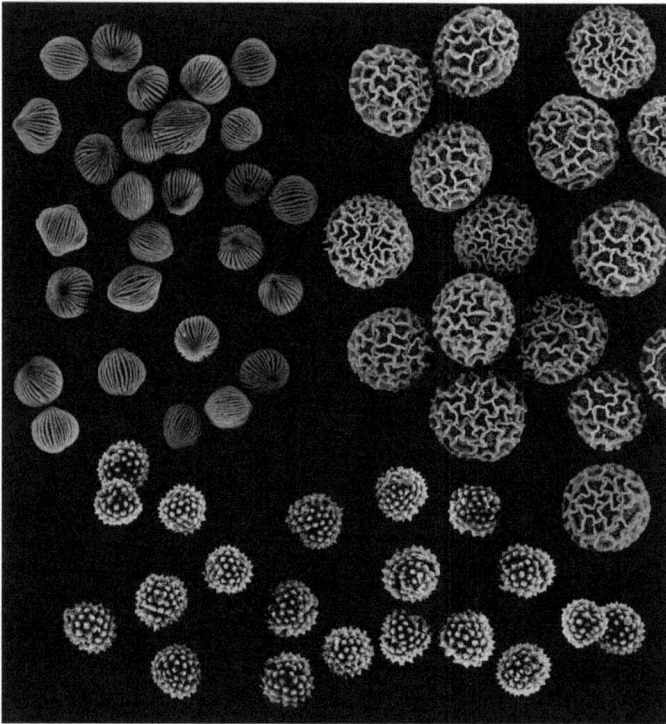

Fig. 1. Three kinds of pollen grains under an electron micrograph: false-colored *Passiflora* (passion vine), *Spathiphyllum* (peace lily), and *Aster* (daisy). Image taken by Asja Radja. CC BY 4.0.

are winged, some sticky, and others explode in puffy projectile clouds upon touch.

To distinguish between individual pollen grains and see their distinct patterns, we require a microscope (see fig. 1). The tiniest pollen grains, those of the forget-me-not (*Myosotis spp.*), measure only 0.005 mm in diameter. What they lack in size, they make up in numbers. While difficult to generalize across species, a flower can produce several tens of thousands of grains. Pollen appears in such quantities to increase the odds of reproduction, since, just as with humans, most sperm cells never reach an egg. Their small size and large number make them look like an undifferentiated powdery substance, or dust, to the naked eye, and this is reflected in language. Pollen is an uncountable or mass noun in English, and the study of pollen is literally the study of dust: palynology. This field matters beyond understanding plant reproduction, since these sturdy little passengers travel not only across space, but also through time. Pollen has been found in the fossil record dating back to over 400 million years ago, and it has helped humans understand the evolution of biodiversity, elucidated historical ways of living, and even solved murders. So-called "pollen fingerprints" have been used to tie evidence to people and places. Since pollen holds such clues about the environment and our history, it is important to disciplines as varied as archaeology, climatology, paleontology, and forensics.

Yet in modern everyday life, most human-pollen encounters are involuntary, aside from its popularity as a health food, and only noticed when they result in an allergic reaction. Nineteenth-century doctors were the first to diagnose allergies like "hay fever," a misleading name, since it is neither caused by hay nor manifests as a fever. Officially called allergic rhinitis, this mostly seasonal physical response to high pollen counts—but also to dust mites, animal dander, mold spores, and other pollutants—has been on the rise since the early twentieth century, when the first scratch tests for pollen allergies were developed. If allergies are increasing, this is at least partly because pollen is too. Pollen counts have been going up in urban environments due to the tendency of city planners to plant male trees, which avoids problems with fruit falling on heads, cars, and sidewalks. Yet this also means that pollen is not absorbed by female trees and left roaming the streets to enter human noses instead. This self-made allergy problem demonstrates that we often seem to forget or ignore what pollen is and does. As a miniscule sperm delivery mechanism, it is all about sex. Accordingly, pollen's cultural history has predominantly been focused on attraction rather than allergic aversion, and because of that, pollen has shaped not only our understanding of plant fertility, but also human ideas about eroticism and sexuality, reproduction and desire.

A History of Pollen, or Flowers Not Keeping It in Their Plants

Talk of "the birds and the bees" may be a favorite euphemism for sex education, but it does not quite make sense as a description of the reproductive act. The German language refers instead to the "bees and flowers" (*die Bienchen und Blümchen*), which clarifies that this shorthand for The Sex Talk is actually about pollination. But bees are not the only pollinators out there. When humans look at and smell flowers, we are attracted by the same enticing color palette and varied scents as other pollinating animals and might accidentally deliver a sperm package to the next flower we stick our nose in. The beauty and sensually pleasing qualities of flowers are, in fact, such successful evolutionary strategies for plant survival that they have prompted the creation of entire industries and inspired plenty of poetry. Yet this floral fascination acquires an erotically charged subtext and potentially uncomfortable innuendo when we remember the reproductive purpose of flowers and relate it to our own sexuality. In other words, smelling flowers might no longer be innocent according to human standards of morality when it is reframed as a nose penetrating plant genitals, or plant sperm entering the human body.

You can perhaps imagine the scandal when someone first suggested a few centuries ago that plants might be sexual beings. For the longest time, plants were thought to reproduce asexually only. When botanists did discuss the idea of plant sexes, they generally posited the existence of just one, female, and conjectured that both women and plants experience a passive, sort of sexless sexuality. Some even suggested immaculate conception in plants, akin to the Virgin Mary, whose innocence is commonly represented by a white lily. Against the backdrop of these ideas, countless love poems coyly compared women to flowers, and the act of compromising someone's chastity was accordingly called defloration. When scientists discovered in the late seventeenth century that pollen was not a form of menstrual but male discharge, this virtuous vision of the sexless female plant was eviscerated. And when Swedish botanist Carl Linnaeus popularized his taxonomy of plants according to their sexual organs in the first half of the eighteenth century, it caused moral outrage across the sciences and society. Linnaeus showed plants to have twenty-four different sex combinations, in addition to multiple ways of achieving sexual and asexual reproduction, and he did so with marriage metaphors, calling flower parts brides and grooms. These ideas were further popularized by Erasmus Darwin, the grandfather of Charles, who wrote "The Loves of Plants" (1789), a poem that illustrates Linnaeus's sexual system by anthropomorphizing plants. Darwin emphasized Linnaeus's sexual descriptions and translated these discoveries from Latin by coining new botanical terms, such as stamen and pistil, which he presented as the vegetal equivalent of penis and vagina.

By showing that plants can reproduce with themselves, change sexes, and contain simultaneously male and female genitals, Linnaeus's work threatened the period's heteronormative standard of married monogamy. His human-plant comparisons and the discovery that a range of sexual behaviors of the supposedly amoral kind were, in fact, natural rendered botany itself a risqué subject. The matter was further complicated by botany's status as one of the only sciences at this time that included work by women and as an increasingly popular pastime among ladies of means and education. Not only did plants as metaphors for women betray the previous world order with their active sexuality, but women themselves were learning about the promiscuous ways of these pollinating perverts. William Polwhele, an eighteenth-century Cornish clergyman, described his concern about women botanists in the satirical poem "The Unsex'd Females": "With bliss botanic as their bosoms heave, / Still pluck forbidden fruit, with mother Eve, / For puberty in signing florets pant, / Or point the prostitution of a plant; / Dissect its organ of unhallow'd lust, / And fondly gaze the titillating dust" (1798,

8–9). These metaphors are rich with salacious innuendo, as women, now likened to the temptress Eve instead of the Virgin Mary, pursue the forbidden knowledge of pollination by lusting for the study of "plant prostitution," "puberty," sexual organs, and specifically the "titillating dust" of pollen.

The notion of botany as a threat to morality ebbed and flowed throughout the next centuries, though figures like Polwhele were ultimately caricatured, for instance in the short story "The Petition" (1904) by German author Hanns Heinz Ewers. In this humorous satire, a Catholic priest discovers a scandalous subject in Bavarian schools: "'Botany!' he yelled wildly. 'Botany!' He recollected himself immediately and regretted his unbecoming eruption. [...] And very, very gently, but with an unbelievable hatred in his voice, he added, 'Botany!'" (Ewers 1919, 115, my translation). The priest is horrified that "young souls are forced" to learn about pollination in schools, where "the teacher leads the pure minds into a hotbed of sin, to a Sodom of the most egregious perversions," since the "entire instruction of botany is solely tailored to the observation of the disgusting practice of [the plants'] sexual functions!" (Ewers 1919, 118). This diatribe is part of a petition against the botany curriculum that the priest sends to the ministry of education. He believes that keeping young people ignorant of all reproductive knowledge will prevent premarital sex and pregnancy, an idea that prevails in our own times, even if we may not recognize botany as a potential culprit. Ironically, the priest describes plant parts, like stamen and pistil, and forms of reproduction, like cross- and self-fertilization, with such a level of detail and botanical accuracy that his petition ends up reproducing the very knowledge he wants to ban. We might take the priest's endeavor to be a comical invention, but Ewers's story was, in fact, satirizing actual curricular censorship of biology education in Germany around 1900. For a quarter of a century, this "botany ban" prohibited topics ranging from ecology to evolutionary theory in German secondary schools because they contradicted the teachings of the church.

While Polwhele was concerned with preserving female virtue, the priest focuses on keeping innocent children away from the study of botany. Comparing pollination to sinful seduction and sex work, his petition casts blame on flowers, which lure insects with their color, scent, and sugar. After describing that teachers unabashedly explain "how the bugs, bees, bumblebees, after they have smeared themselves in one blossom with the male pollen, now fly on to the next blossom to wipe off the disgusting powder on the female pistil there and pollinate it this way," the priest exclaims, "Truly, even in a brothel you could not entertain more abominable conversations!" (Ewers 1919, 119). In this complicated interspecies threesome of pollination, flowers appear simultaneously as sex workers and customers, while seducing and also paying insects for "pandering" (Ewers 1919, 119). The priest's worries over botany's corruption of the youth seems to be warranted when the children assume the role of bees in a local chestnut pollination campaign, for which they receive sandwiches and coffee as "pandering *reward,* just like the insects" (Ewers 1919, 122). Rather than "smearing" their bodies with pollen, the children "break off big twigs with blossoms and march through the forest, jubilating and singing," and with a similar gusto as the bees, "they beat with their twigs into the blossoming branches of the trees, to perform the act of pollination" (Ewers 1919, 122). This quasi-orgiastic, somewhat violent, and certainly erotically charged act of pleasure is made even more explicit when drawing on another of Ewers's stories, in which the scent of chestnut blossoms is associated with that of semen, or "eternally victorious masculinity" (Ewers 1912, 156, my translation).

According to the Catholic priest, the pollinating insects and children participate in a process that is meant to be about reproduction, not pleasure—priorities that are reversed in his depiction of pollination as sex work. Non-reproductive pleasure also suggests the possibility of broadening strictly heteronormative understandings of sex. The priest ranks the plants' morality according to their apparent conformity with monogamous heterosexuality. As he summarizes the Linnean system in the petition, he notes that "[M]onandria, plants with one female and one male genital" seem to be "the only half decent plants" (Ewers

1919, 120). In all other categories, male and female genitals multiply or merge, and the priest's strict morality is quite upset by
this natural diversity of sexes and paths to reproduction. Beyond his worry about sexual pleasure outside of marriage, these
passages make room for sexual encounters across sexes and
even between different species. In Ewers's time, sexual freedom
and possibilities were, in fact, increasing. With the emergence
of early sexology at this time, many sexual identities and orientations were first officially named, studied, and managed to rise
to the social surface in short-lived liberal bubbles such as Wei-
mar Germany's interwar Berlin. Though human sexuality and
plant pollination do not always align, the sensual attraction of
colorful, pollen-dusted blossoms with their enticing scents and
the plants' natural bouquet of varied sexual options suggested
then and now that the experience of diverse kinds of pleasures
is natural.

Pleasure is why plants pose a "danger to morality" (Ewers
1919, 117). Though pollen's purpose is reproductive, plants seem
to expend a big portion of their resources on seducing everyone
around them. While the industrious image of the "bustling, busy
bee" carrying golden pollen kernels suggests an economic process of great efficiency that turns reproduction into production
and recalls the financial side of sex work, pollen's excesses tell a
different story. Getting sperm to the egg is a gamble, dependent
on the whims of wind and water, or the flight path of pollinators. This inefficient dispersion necessitates excessive numbers
and expects a high rate of failure. Inefficiency is why the floral
attraction of pollinators through pleasurable colors and scent is
so important. Seduction therefore becomes the main focus of
the sexual process, even though this is not the moment of fertilization and might not lead to any reproductive success. Pollen
suggests excess instead of economy, failure instead of functional
fruitfulness, and pleasurable appeals to the senses instead of
purposive exertion.

Fig. 2. Diadasia bee straddles *Opuntia engelmannii* cactus flower carpels. Close-up taken by Jessie Eastland. CC BY-SA 4.0.

Golden Delight and Returning to Dust

While a pollen-gilded flower can symbolize life itself by way of reproduction, it also represents the passage of time through the changing of seasons and the ephemerality of beauty, desire, and existence. In our age of mass extinctions, close-up views of velvety bees covered in golden pollen grains (see fig. 2) urge us to pay attention to the entanglement with and dependence of all life on its smallest contributors. The golden richness of pollen as a sign of life and its simultaneous fragility has received predominantly poetic adoration—allergies be damned. Since most pollen is yellow, its color is typically associated with the sun as the source of photosynthesis, and hence the origin of life, and, beyond honey, with nectar, the drink of the gods. American poet Ross Gay takes up this divine notion and offers prayers to a lily, the flower representing the Virgin Mary, in his *Book of Delights* (2019):

> I pray to [the lily] daily in the four to six weeks that it offers up its pinkish speckling by getting on my knees and pushing my face in, which, yes, is also a kind of kissing, [...] the flower kissing [...] will in fact kill you with delight, will annihilate you with delight, will end the life you had previously led before kneeling here and breathing the breathing thing's breath, and the lily will resurrect you too, your lips and nose lit with gold dust, your face and fingers smelling faintly all day of where they've been, amen. (70–71)

The sacred act of "getting on my knees" mingles with an erotic encounter of "kissing" the lily's "pinkish speckling" and "pushing my face in" that evokes cunnilingus. Pollen's "gold dust" becomes the lingering mark of the act, "your face and fingers smelling faintly all day of where they've been." In Gay's prayer to the lily, pollen becomes ornament and sign, gilding and anointing the worshipper like a bee, while the pleasure of *la petite mort,* the sensation after orgasm that is likened to death, resurrects him to a new life, through annihilation and immaculate rebirth. Pollen's reproductive purpose suggests a cyclical opportunity for starting over, yet this new life is more than a biological beginning. It is the rebirth to living in pleasure, or in the words of Gay's book title, delight.

The poet "breathing the thing's breath" reminds us that plants, as the producers of oxygen, are life-givers and sustainers, even if the ephemerality of flowers is a common symbol of the brevity and end of life. By association, life's beginnings and endings are also inscribed into pollen. German poet Rainer Maria Rilke correlates floral and human finitude in his short poem "The Flower of Farewell" from 1924. This flower "blooms, and scatters perpetual pollen" and "we breathe it," and in breathing pollen, "we breathe farewell" (Rilke 2011, 261). Just as the blooming flower is ephemeral, the grains may not have reached their intended destination. The inhaled pollen travels through our body instead and is incorporated, becoming part of us. Thinking of our porous, permeable, and penetrated materiality troubles the unified understanding of the human self, but it is an important reminder of our kinship with even the smallest of matter, and a sense of life beyond the individual. Not only do pollen particles become a part of ourselves, but ultimately, we ourselves return to dust.

Dust is a mixture of various microscopically small matter that is more often rejected as an allergen, pollutant, and simply dirt rather than being poetically revered as a golden ornament—if it is noticed at all. Yet Ross Gay's poetic veneration of pollen as "gold dust" resonates with the German term for pollen, *Blütenstaub* or "blossom dust." Dust consists of everything, covers everything, is nearly everywhere, and can get into everything, often unnoticed. It is diffuse in its content, and diffusion is its form, which gives it plentiful potential, as the many different ways of achieving plant reproduction also show. Yet this is precisely why pollen causes anxiety too. Dust cannot be kept out or controlled easily, and while pollen is a sign of life, it is simultaneously also inscribed with a reminder of its end. Pollen's existence in excess and with dubious reproductive efficacy directs our focus on the pleasures of the here and now, even if that entails failure. That is the threat perceived by the priest and the potential adored by the poet.

References and Further Reading

Bell, Karen L., Berry Brosi, and Kevin Burgess. 2016. "Pollen Genetics Can Help with Forensic Investigations." *The Conversation*. September 5. https://theconversation. com/pollen-genetics-can-help-with-forensic-investigations-53426.

Browne, Janet. 1989. "Botany for Gentlemen: Erasmus Darwin and *The Loves of the Plants*." *Isis* 80, no. 4: 593–621. DOI: 10.1086/355166.

Connelly, Tristanne. 2016. "Flowery Porn: Form and Desire in Erasmus Darwin's *The Loves of the Plants*." *Literature Compass* 13, no. 10: 604–16. DOI: 10.1111/lic3.12347.

Ewers, Hanns Heinz. 1912. "Aus dem Tagebuch eines Orangenbaumes." In *Das Grauen*, 135–70. Munich: Georg Müller.

———. 1919. "Die Petition." In *Der gekreuzigte Tannhäuser und andere Grotesken*, 109–24. Munich: Georg Müller.

Fara, Patricia. 2003. *Sex, Botany, and Empire: Carl Linnaeus and Joseph Banks*. London: Icon Books Limited.

Farley, John. 1982. *Gametes and Spores: Ideas about Sexual Reproduction 1750–1914*. Baltimore: Johns Hopkins University Press.

Gay, Ross. 2019. *The Book of Delights*. Chapel Hill: Algonquin Books.

George, Sam. 2007. *Botany, Sexuality, and Women's Writing, 1760–1830: From Modest Shoot to Forward Plant*. Manchester: Manchester University Press.

George, Sam, and Alison E. Martin, eds. 2011. "Woman and Botany." Special issue of *Journal of Literature and Science* 4, no. 1. https://www.literatureandscience.org/volume-4-issue-1/.

Haskell, David George. 2013. "Nature's Case for Same-Sex Marriage." *The New York Times*, March 30. http://www. nytimes.com/2013/03/30/opinion/natures-case-for-same-sex-marriage.html.

Heinemann, Caspar. 2016. "Fucking Pansies: Queer Poetics, Plant Reproduction, Plant Poetics, Queer Reproduction." BA Thesis, Goldsmiths, University of London. https://www.academia.edu/32408905/FUCKING_PANSIES_Queer_Poetics_Plant_Reproduction_Plant_Poetics_Queer_Reproduction.

Hustak, Carla, and Natasha Myers. 2012. "Involutionary Momentum: Affective Ecologies and the Sciences of Plant/Insect Encounters." *differences* 23, no. 3: 74–118. DOI: 10.1215/10407391-1892907.

Jacobs, Joela. 2016. "Plant Parenthood: The Fear of Vegetal Eroticism." In *Imperceptibly and Slowly Opening,* edited by Caroline Picard, 166–72. Chicago: The Green Lantern Press.

———. 2019. "Phytopoetics: Upending the Passive Paradigm with Vegetal Violence and Eroticism." *Catalyst* 5, no. 2: 1–18. DOI: 10.28968/cftt.v5i2.30027.

———. 2022. "'These Lusting, Incestuous, Perverse Creatures': A Phytopoetic History of Plants and Sexuality." *Environmental Humanities* 14, no. 3: 602–17. DOI: 10.1215/22011919-9962926.

Kelley, Theresa M. 2012. *Clandestine Marriage: Botany and Romantic Culture.* Baltimore: Johns Hopkins University Press.

Kessler, Rob, and Madeline Harley. 2004. *Pollen: The Hidden Sexuality of Flowers.* London: Papadakis Publishers.

MacPhail, Theresa. 2016. "Irritated: A Historical Overview of Allergies." *LA Review of Books,* March 10. https://lareviewofbooks.org/article/irritated-a-historical-overview-of-allergies/.

Mortimer-Sandilands, Catriona, and Bruce Erickson. 2010. *Queer Ecologies: Sex, Nature, Politics, Desire.* Bloomington: Indiana University Press.

Ogren, Thomas Leo. 2003. *Safe Sex in the Garden and Other Propositions for an Allergy-Free World.* Berkeley: Ten Speed Press.

Polwhele, Richard. 1798. *The Unsex'd Females: A Poem, Addressed to the Author of the Pursuits of Literature.* London: Cadell and Davies.

Sandford, Stella. 2022. *Vegetal Sex: Philosophy of Plants.* London: Bloomsbury.

Schiebinger, Londa. 1993. *Nature's Body: Gender in the Making of Modern Science.* Boston: Beacon Press.

Rilke, Rainer Maria. 2011. *Selected Poems.* Edited by Robert Vilain. Translated by Marielle Sutherland and Susan Ranson. Oxford: Oxford University Press.

Shteir, Ann B. 1996. *Cultivating Women, Cultivating Science: Flora's Daughters and Botany in England, 1760–1860.* Baltimore: Johns Hopkins University Press.

Sommerey, Constance. 2014. "'Illegal Science': The Case of Ernst Haeckel (1834–1919) and German Biology Education." *Shells and Pebbles,* August 4. http://www.shellsandpebbles. com/2014/08/04/illegal-science-the-case-of-ernst-haeckel-1834-1919-and-german-biology-education/.

Taiz, Lincoln, and Lee Taiz. 2017. *Flora Unveiled: The Discovery and Denial of Sex in Plants.* Oxford: Oxford University Press.

CHAPTER 7

Protozoa

Dani Lamorte

Protozoa, noun: a unicellular life form which is neither animal, nor plant, nor fungus; has a proper nucleus and often has no capacity for photosynthesis.

As definitions go, this one seems to hide more than it reveals. We might as well define the sky as blue but neither a bird nor a stocking nor an aristocrat, and totally lacking in salacious innuendo. But let's be patient with the imprecision above. Defining protozoa is no simple task. In his 2003 guide to seeing protozoa under a microscope, biologist D.J. Patterson writes that "protozoa cannot be easily defined [...]; measured in molecular terms, two protozoa may have less in common than do a plant and an animal" (Patterson 2003, 9–10). Protozoa are defined by exclusion. Unlike plants, most protozoans, a term which catches protozoa-y creatures, do not photosynthesize. Unlike animals, protozoans are not multicellular. Unlike fungi, protozoans do not emerge from spores. R.W. Sanders, contemporary to Patterson, describes the protist — the category that encompasses the taxonomic group of protozoa — as a "term of convenience that describes an assemblage of often distantly related organisms lumped together as a matter of ecological utility" (Sanders 2009, 56). As a linguistic organism, a thing that lives in our symbols and speech, protozoa may be defined as a planned identity crisis, a taxonomical landfill. Like the towering yet crumbling heaps at the edges of our cities, the category of protozoa is a site of disarray that makes it possible for the domestic and public categories of plant and animal to appear meaningfully different, discrete. If we don't know quite what protozoa is, all the better.

German zoologist Georg A. Goldfuss first dubbed these unicellular organisms protozoa in 1817. Forty-three years later, British anatomist Sir Richard Owen adopted the term for his taxonomical work and provided the following etymology for protozoa — *proto-* coming from the Greek for "first" and *-zoē* meaning "life." Whether or not protozoans came first in a sequence of evolutionary forms and how that firstness relates to the eventual arrival of human beings was not widely agreed upon then and is far from settled now. Tellingly, Owens also floated the name *acrita,* coming from the Greek for "indiscernible." The logic of finding firsts would be used later by German zoologist Ernst Haeckel who coined the term protist, meaning "the very first," for the category that now *includes* protozoa. A modern use of these terms might be that protists are unicellular life forms with a proper nucleus that are neither animal, plant, nor fungus. Protozoa are protists that do not photosynthesize, usually. Simultaneously narrow and ambiguous, some consider the category of protozoa problematic or obsolete. See also: protoctista, protean.

It is tempting to tease the biological from the linguistic, to fix the image of the "real" creature under our microscopes and relegate the question of names to a second order of less-real abstraction. However, the practice of biology is mired in these monikers and metrics, in the asking and answering of "what is that?" and its twin inquiry, "what am I looking for?" The names we have encountered so far suggest that we are seeking in these little creatures the very first, the original. We are seeking the earliest impressions of life on our planet, from a time when life was one single entity. We are seeking the time before species. Studies in prehistoric biology try to answer questions about when and where *we* came from. Writing that history would be simple if we could consciously remember our evolution, but we cannot, and this gap in our knowledge, which perhaps feels like a forgetting, is a trouble science resolves to resolve. As a word, protozoa indicates a moment when science slid a mirror under the lens of a microscope, hoping to look back behind us, through us. In this glance, we inaugurate the category of "first life," both a point of origin and a record of something we have surpassed. With an eye to the cyclical practices of terminology and taxonomy, a new definition for protozoa might be an instability caused by a failure to remember, a trouble with knowing.

Protozoan Doings

If there is one group of protozoans you already know, it is probably amoebae. Amoeba forms its plural following the Latin rules of grammar, resulting in amoebae, pronounced uh-mee-bee, as though the first vowel were lifting the second into its realm. Amoebae are unicellular life forms lacking a defined shape or, colloquially, blobs. Many amoebae engulf prey with temporary protuberances called pseudopodia, or fake feet, and guide their neighbor-turned-nosh towards mouth-like cytostomes. Some move with rudder-like flagella. Living in soils and freshwaters, amoebae are globally plentiful. They are counted by water sanitation experts, collected by ecologists, cultivated by biological supply companies, and spun and genetically sequenced by laboratory machines. Amoebae are also placed into narrative structures by biologists, perhaps with the hope of discovering that amoebas have a "society" like ours, and perhaps there is something natural about society after all. Amoeboid biographies come with the headings familiar to Wikipedians: Early Life, Works, Death. Canny readers look for another heading: Personal Life. Labyrinthine encounters characterize protozoa in the micro-world. For example, some bacteria and viruses have evolved mechanisms for surviving the hungry gulp of an amoeba. Stopping the transition from ingestion to digestion, these microorganisms take up residence within the amoeba's cellular membranes. Inside the predator-turned-host, these organisms exchange genetic material and take shelter from harsh conditions. When conditions are right, the viruses or bacteria will exit the amoeba, and, if the amoeba itself happened to be ensconced within a host, begin infecting animal or plant cells. Relationships between protozoan and non-protozoan organisms can also turn symbiotic, with some protozoans "stealing" energy from photosynthesizing organisms. Some botanists hypothesize, or fantasize, that photosynthesis in plants evolved as the result of a protozoa-like organism forming a symbiotic relationship with photosynthetic cyanobacteria, often called blue-green algae.

Toxoplasma gondii, the parasitic protozoan that causes toxoplasmosis, might also be well-known to those of us with feline companions, as it sexually reproduces only within the guts of cats. Viewed through a microscope, *T. gondii* is often stained violet and appears as a field of pudgy commas. In an absurdist take on the Cinderella story, *T. gondii* infects mice and transforms them into vehicles by permanently inhibiting the rodent's instinctive aversion to cat scents. The newly emboldened mouse is soon within the jaws of a hungry cat, and *T. gondii* is well on its way to its desired destination. *Nosema granulosis,* an amoeba-like microorganism, retools its host in other ways, and it spreads intergenerationally through *Gammarus duebeni* shrimp by catching a ride on the female shrimp's eggs. If a fertilized egg begins to develop as a male, this presents a dead end for *N. granulosis,* since it requires a female shrimp with eggs to host its next generation. In response, *N. granulosis* will change the sex of the developing shrimp from male to female and thereby ensure its own continuation. *N. granulosis* got what it gave when it was recategorized by biologists as a microsporidian, a relative of fungi, rather than a protozoan. *N. granulosis* and *T. gondii* live by opening and closing channels of affect and identity in other creatures by making predators seem friendly and turning potential rivals into potential mates. The *I* in "I want this" or "I fear this" becomes more vague. Where does the desire for someone or something specific originate? In tracing the protozoan moves of *N. granulosis* and *T. gondii,* we find that the forms taken by desire are not shaped by a singular self-driving entity but are given dimension and orientation by multiple agents.

These pluralistic amoeboid imaginings might take the form of a utopian, ecological fantasy, were amoebas not also a hazard to our very thinking. The amoeba *Naegleria fowleri,* known popularly as brain-eating amoeba, exemplifies this best. *N. fowleri* enters the human brain via nerves deep in the nasal cavity and begins to consume brain tissue. The body's immune response exacerbates the damage, combining tissue destruction with brain swelling. For most humans infected by *N. fowleri,* death occurs within twelve days. *N. fowleri* destroys the taxonomizing mind for the infected human and pushes protozoa beyond being a confused category towards being a meaningless string of sounds. Insultingly, *N. fowleri* is not even particularly interested in our brains. It is just an opportunistic feeder who would rather be in its freshwater home. Another genus, *Acanthamoeba,* offends the human eye rather than the brain. *Acanthamoeba* enters the cornea of the eye through a damaged spot and begins to consume healthy tissue, in some cases suppressing immune reactions along the way. Despite being closer to the eye than ever, despite now being in direct contact with the human optical system, *Acanthamoeba* remains invisible to us. Left untreated, *Acanthamoeba* infection leads to blindness.

It feels easy, sometimes, to peer at protozoa from on high, looking through our technological gizmos to reveal, or hide, something about the world. But when they infect us, whether a literal infection or an infection of uncertainty about what it is we are talking about, protozoa bring us down to earth. The mythos of evolutionary history tells the tale of intrepid hominids rising up out of the protozoan muck towards the shimmering stars and, along the way, transcending the muddy qualities of life through language, philosophy, art, technology, and, most notably, science. When we are felled by protozoa, we inhabit the domain proper to the earthworms, spiders, spit, entities that French philosopher Georges Bataille described as *l'informe,* formless. In his one-paragraph essay of the same name, Bataille wonders about these creatures along the horizontal axis, taking a route different than the rising humanoid column. For Bataille, the conceit and calamity of human beings is their evolution from horizontal forms, close to the earth, to a vertical vertebrate animal which, at different times and in diverse ways, imagines itself at the center of things. That which is *l'informe*, formless, is that which does not affirm the sense of accomplishment we invest into our erect stature. Instead, spiders and spit are "squashed everywhere" (Bataille 1985, 31), with an indifference not towards the actual squashing, but towards the possibility of *not* being squashed. In other words, formless creatures are immune to the allure of a future defined by success, by being remembered. Maybe spiders do not really feel this way, but in their lowness Bataille saw the opportunity to wonder about these non-aspirational impulses. Art historian Yve-Alain Bois suggests we think of "formless" not so much as a quality that a creature, say, an amoeba, possesses but instead as an operation. If something is formless, it acts to "horizontalize" the mind and bring life back to an unmetered pit of consumption and excretion, and no more the great build-up of evolution or the ever-rising intellect of man, but a base fecundity without culmination. Thinking about protozoa necessitates a willingness to fall, from the heights of human scientific accomplishment and from our identities, to a sort of death of our hubris, and perhaps not get back up. Protozoa is a symbol of our lives as porous but not indistinct. Through a willingness to fall, we see the possibilities contained within the words and beings we have bound together: being done to (like protozoans studied in labs) and doing to (like *N. fowleri* consuming our brains), being done inside of (like amoebae hosting viruses) and doing inside of (like *T. Gondii* driving rodent vehicles). Protozoa is about seeking *ad hoc* opportunity, changing the terms of the game for short-term benefit without the promise of escaping punishment. Holding the linguistic and biological together, protozoa — a thing of firstness, a thing to be superseded, a shape of life — can be defined as the creation of temporary fantasies about origins of the self, of the species. These self-conscious fantasies do not indicate the sincere belief that an origin exists or can be found but pursue fantasy for pleasure. Any "true origins" of our species or selves would prove less desirable, less poetic than our fantasies, and the dream itself is doomed since returning to the horizontal fully is impossible, though no more so than becoming fully "vertical." The dream is doomed. Pursue it anyway, and watch it collapse. Then, dream again. Neither scientific positivism nor dogmatic spiritualism, protozoa, a bundle of hope to find the first, calls for the continuation of desire without insisting on knowing where that desire leads, or that it leads anywhere in particular, or that where it leads is true.

A Foil and a Puncture

Lynda Benglis's *Contraband* (1969) and Anne Truitt's *Summer Treat* (1968) are two works of art through which we might try our hand, or our eye, at thinking about protozoa. Both works were created in the late 1960s, and both are sometimes called a sculpture, but Benglis and Truitt thought very differently about what it is they were making and why. Like the species within the category of protozoa, these two works can only tentatively be categorized together as a temporary convenience that is always falling apart.

Contraband (fig. 1) is an irregular shape of poured rubber latex, hand-pigmented with Day-Glo™ colors and measuring nearly 9.5 feet by 33 feet (approximately 2.95 meters by 10 meters) at its extremities. Created in 1969 for an exhibit at the Whitney Museum of American Art in New York City, the work is a floor-pour painting, meaning Benglis created it by pouring the latex directly onto the studio or gallery floor. Roughly 1.5 inches (0.3 centimeters) tall, the work requires the viewer's gaze to fall down and spread wide like the poured latex itself. Like Bataille's spiders and spit, *Contraband* stretches out horizontally and, when installed in a gallery, comes ever closer to the dirt and dust and shit and sand microscopically tumbling from the shoes of museum visitors. *Contraband*'s ground-ward fall is con-

Fig. 1. Contraband (1969) by Lynda Benglis. Poured latex. Approx. 2.95 m × 10 m × 0.3 cm. © 2023 Lynda Benglis. Licensed by VAGA at Artists Rights Society (ARS), New York.

tinued by the downward trajectory of these particles. Your feet, not your eyes, get closest to the work.

In an interview, Benglis explains:

> I think my interest in materials is very contextual and has not so much to do with the expression, but it has really to do with my learning what the materials are and what they can do, in relationship to art history and contextually in relationship to the environment, the room, the wall, the floor. (Whitney Museum of American Art 2009)

Benglis's focus on materials reveals to us the steps of the process, the individual chemical components involved, and the industrial and consumer context of her media. In interviews, vivid descriptions of her process reveal a time when *Contraband* was liquid, and its parameters were not yet set. As a work from an artist who focuses on materials rather than gestures or representations, there is something amoeboid and protozoan, something original, about *Contraband*. Other colors could have been mixed in Benglis's studio, another carrier medium selected, another method of application chosen. As the latex fell towards the floor, the possible permutations were not unlimited, but chance was still at play.

Contraband suggests protean memories, echoes from a time before the latex cured into its more permanent exhibition form. It is delicious to fantasize about these "lost moments," these other potential forms. Is this not something like fantasizing about the first life *like us* to emerge on Earth? Through science, we obsess over naming and knowing, and continually seek the unifying evidence to explain *it* all. Somewhere inside our search, I think, lurks a hope that learning where "we," whatever that might mean, come from will be just like being there when it all took place.

Contraband was originally created for an exhibition at the Whitney Museum, but its unexpectedly large size and shockingly bright colors made curators unsure how to install the piece. They suggested displaying it in the entrance to the museum, flowing up onto a ramp and away from the foot traffic. Benglis objected to the idea of *Contraband* leaving the floor and to her work being shown in the less-prestigious foyer while other artists took up the vaunted galleries. As a woman working in high art at mid-century, Benglis's second complaint is patently reasonable. More generally, however, protozoa can help us see a tension between these two complaints. On one hand, she objects to *Contraband* leaving the floor, a traditionally ignored, if not loathed location in the museum. On the other hand, she finds in the museum entrance a space that is lower than the floor, a commercial, non-aesthetic space still beneath her. Thinking

Fig. 2. Summer Treat (1968) by Anne Truitt (1921–2004). Latex paint on wood (sculpture). Approx. 280 cm × 61 cm × 61 cm. Collection of The University of Arizona Museum of Art, Tucson. Gift of Mrs. James Angleton. © Estate of Anne Truitt. All rights reserved 2023/Bridgeman Images.

protozoa is hard to take all the way to its conclusion: just when we are ready to get down, get low, get dirty, we remember how far we have to fall, and we catch ourselves. The visual metaphor of the blobby, curvy amoeba easily engulfs amorphous artwork like *Contraband,* though we should remember that the "likeness" of protozoa is based on not actually being like anything in particular. To think about protozoa with courage, we have to set our sights on vertical, telescopic beings, beings like Anne Truitt's *Summer Treat.*

A tall square column of creamy yellow-orange with a light golden sand ring around its lower margin, *Summer Treat* (fig. 2) is a work of sculpture often classified as "minimalist" or "abstract," though Truitt rebuffed both monikers. My first impressions of *Summer Treat* were those of an interesting architectural detail, or a whim of interior design. A cosmetic, commercial thing. A utilitarian object. A means of directing traffic. In my initial encounter with the work at the University of Arizona Museum of Art, I first mistook *Summer Treat* for part of the room. I read the sculpture as the backdrop against which art is presented, not art itself. It stood, plain yet beautiful, towards the center of the room, and it seemed to coordinate effortlessly with the wall paint and gallery lighting. Its base, smaller than the rest of the structure and recessed away from the eye, gave it a floating quality. A few seconds into my visual exploration of the column, I noticed a didactic label, which identified *Summer Treat* as an artwork on display, and I laughed. It is a joy to mistake a mundane object for art and to mistake art for the mundane.

Truitt's columns are akin to bodies. In a 1987 interview, the artist explains, "[t]he line of gravity runs as the center of every one of my sculptures. In the same way that a line of gravity runs through the center of a person from the top of the person's head down to the feet" (quoted in Dawson 1987). The color of each work, she continues, is "magnetically" drawn to that center of gravity. In Jem Cohen's short 2009 film on Truitt, the artist describes her work as creating fields of living color that are "liberated" into space along this vertical gravitational axis. *Summer Treat* does not rise towards a field of limitless possibilities but is rather in a predetermined ascension along the line that gives it meaning. Although Truitt says she places these works on feet, just as she stands on feet, *Summer Treat's* feet are hidden. The work rises up up up towards its preordained transcendence, and, if *Summer Treat* were to look down, it would not see its feet buried in the muddy muck of the earth. Flying sunward, the sculpture is a mind of shining color attempting to escape its body.

Although Truitt had something particular in mind when she created *Summer Treat,* no work of art escapes the possibility of being read otherwise. In the sculpture's colors and shape, I read other, less philosophical meanings. Where Truitt lifted color along a vertical axis to liberate it, I saw a commercial, interchangeable thing — standing tall, yes, but without significance. When I laughed, at my ignorance and foolish certainty, the laugh marked an inversion of high and low. The didactic text next to *Summer Treat* raised the column from the category of building materials to the category of art in my awareness, and it simultaneously lowered me, via embarrassment, towards being an *ignoramus,* a Philistine. The laughter that marked the beginning of my understanding of *Summer Treat* as art performed a protozoan operation, destabilizing taxonomies of objects. If I cannot tell art from *things,* how can I tell *things* from myself? A similar laughter erupted from me when I first saw protozoa under a microscope, suddenly there, where nothing had been! Protozoa became terribly real in that moment, and I felt like a thin fiction, a lie told to myself. A whole microscopic world bustles around me, and I am not made for perceiving it, perhaps even for thinking about it. Not only do the eyes lie at times, but they are also terribly uninformed. As I try to know protozoa, the sense of trying becomes strained and straining. In the end, I do not know what protozoa is except something I want to know.

The function of intellect is to "settle" this laughter and place everything on new levels. I might tell myself that I am correctly evolved for my environmental niche or fault the museum staff for installing *Summer Treat* as they did. Rather than settling these matters and making sense of protozoa, let's look for other less sensible possibilities. Let's fantasize about other possibilities of encountering *Summer Treat* too. What if *Summer Treat* were toppled like a domino, skewing Truitt's rigid axis? From an upright capital "I" to a leaning forward slash "/" leading to other directions, directories, entries, dead ends. In this scenario, the column would never return to standing or lay at rest. No blank spaces ____. As its base lifts from the ground, the veil of shadow is pulled away from the column's feet and we glimpse its point of origin, the point from which it departs the horizontal and reaches for the heights of evolutionary grandeur. As the hidden record of the object's construction and the site of its earthly attachments, these wooden feet would slowly move towards alignment with the top of the sculpture. Never unified but never separate are the face of god, the destroying brilliance, the fetid stench of decay, the shame of the species, and the mind addled by protozoa as pathogen and protozoa as category. Suddenly, the very far away solar palette to which we aspire and the very muddy closeness of which we are embarrassed are pulled into a simultaneity. Just by standing in place, *Summer Treat* becomes the aching possibility of watching it fall. (An ache too powerful, based on the incident when a museum-goer did push one of Truitt's columns over.) Perhaps something similar could be said of the category "human." Do we fret about the boundaries between human and technology, or human and animal, just so we can practice our arguments for what makes the human special? Protozoa, as a knotting of organism and language, intervenes here to suggest letting go of our anxious arguments, letting our past and future fail, not as a prompt for getting it right in another future or past, but as an opportunity to enjoy the vertigo of a fall.

References and Further Reading

Barford, Eliot. 2013. "Parasite Makes Mice Lose Fear of Cats Permanently." *Nature.com,* September 18. https://www.nature.com/news/parasite-makes-mice-lose-fear-of-cats-permanently-1.13777.

Bataille, Georges. 1985. "Formless." In *Visions of Excess: Selected Writings, 1927–1939,* edited by Allan Stoekl, translated by Allan Stoekl, Carl R. Lovitt, and Donald M. Leslie Jr. 31. Minneapolis: University of Minnesota Press.

———. 1985. "The Labyrinth." In *Visions of Excess: Selected Writings, 1927–1939,* edited by Allan Stoekl, translated by Allan Stoekl, Carl R. Lovitt, and Donald M. Leslie Jr., 171–77. Minneapolis: University of Minnesota Press.

Béchard, Dominique. 2016. "Amoeba." *Arc (Ottawa)* 79: 15.

Bois, Yve-Alain. 1997. "The Use Value of 'Formless.'" In Yve-Alain Bois and Rosalind E. Krauss, *Formless: A User's Guide,* 13–42. New York: Zone Books.

Brock, Debra A., Tamara S. Haselkorn, Justine R. Garcia, Usman Bashir, Tracy E. Douglas, Jesse Galloway, Fisher Brodie, David C. Queller, and Joan E. Strassmann. 2018. "Diversity of Free-Living Environmental Bacteria and Their Interactions with a Bactivorous Amoeba." *Frontiers in Cellular and Infection Microbiology* 8: 411. DOI: 10.3389/fcimb.2018.00411.

Brookhardt, D. Eric. 2017. "Lynda Benglis: I Choose My Dreams." *Sculpture: A Publication of the International Sculpture Center,* April 1. https://sculpturemagazine.art/lynda-benglis-i-choose-my-dreams/.

Callenbach, Ernest. 2008. "Protists." In *Ecology: A Pocket Guide,* 109. Berkeley: University of California Press.

Cohen, Jem. 2009. "Anne Truitt, Working." *The Video Databank.* https://vdb.org/titles/anne-truitt-working.

Dawson, Victoria. 1987. "Anne Truitt and the Color of Truth." *The Washington Post,* March 14. https://www.washingtonpost.com/archive/lifestyle/1987/03/14/anne-

truitt-and-the-color-of-truth/feodfb81-4bcf-48e5-8bbd-
7533b3b3e1cb/.

Delafont, Vincent, Amélie Brouke, Didier Bouchon, Laurent
Moulin, and Yann Héchard. 2013. "Microbiome of
Free-Living Amoebae Isolated from Drinking Water."
Water Research 47, no. 19: 6958–65. DOI: 10.1016/j.
watres.2013.07.047.

Delafont, Vincent, Marie-Hélêne Rodier, Elodie Maisonneuve,
and Estelle Cateau. 2018. "*Vermamoeba vermiformis:* A
Free-Living Amoeba of Interest." *Microbial Ecology* 76, no.
4: 991–1001. DOI: 10.1007/s00248-018-1199-8.

Magnet, A., S. Fenoy, A.L. Galván, F. Izquierdo, C. Rueda,
C. Fernandez Vadillo, and C. Del Aguila. 2013. "A Year
Long Study of the Presence of Free Living Amoeba in
Spain." *Water Research* 47, no. 19: 6966–72. DOI: 10.1016/j.
watres.2013.09.065.

Miller, Thomas E., Emma R. Moran, and Casey P. terHorst.
2014. "Rethinking Niche Evolution: Experiments with
Natural Communities of Protozoa in Pitcher Plants." *The
American Naturalist* 184, no. 2: 277–83. DOI: 10.1086/676943.

Patterson, David J. 2003. *Free-living Freshwater Protozoa: A
Colour Guide.* Washington, DC: ASM Press.

Pickett-Heaps, Jeremy, dir. 2006. *The Kingdom Protista.*
Cytographics. https://www.kanopy.com/en/product/238398.

Rothschild, Lynn J. 1989. "Protozoa, Protist, Protoctista: What's
in a Name?" *Journal of the History of Biology* 22, no. 2:
277–305. https://www.jstor.org/stable/4331095.

Sanders, R.W. 2010. "Protists." In *Plankton of Inland Waters: A
Derivative Encyclopedia of Inland Waters,* edited by Gene E.
Likens, 56–64. Amsterdam: Elsevier.

Thomas, Vincent, and Gilbert Greub. 2010. "Amoeba/
Amoebal Symbiont Genetic Transfers: Lessons from Giant
Viral Neighbors." *Intervirology* 53, no. 3: 254–67. DOI:
10.1159/000312910.

Werren, John H. 2003. "Invasion of the Gender-Benders."
Natural History 112, no. 1: 58–63.

Whitney Museum of American Art. 2009. "Whitney Focus
    Presents Lynda Benglis." *YouTube*. https://www.youtube.
    com/watch?v=Yq7VkLUhY18.

CHAPTER 8

Viruses

Raymond Malewitz

Given the COVID-19 global pandemic of 2020–22, it may be challenging to think of viruses as neglected micromatter. After all, though the name for the viral agent that causes COVID-19 (SARS-CoV-2) may be a relatively obscure term, even a child can recognize its image: a spiky protein shell that calls to mind a sea urchin or a naval mine (see fig. 1). Inside that tiny shell is an even tinier single strand of RNA, a set of instructions written in the language of four molecular base pairs. When our cells meet SARS-CoV-2, they read its message and find it so irresistible that they copy it again and again until we are sick of it and begin passing the same message to other people. The resulting cacophony of reading and rewriting has shut down national economies, altered political landscapes, transformed educational systems, and ended millions of human lives. After all the literal and metaphorical reading and rewriting, all of the op-eds and news reports, the social media posts and the pandemic briefings, how could we not pay attention to the lives of viruses?

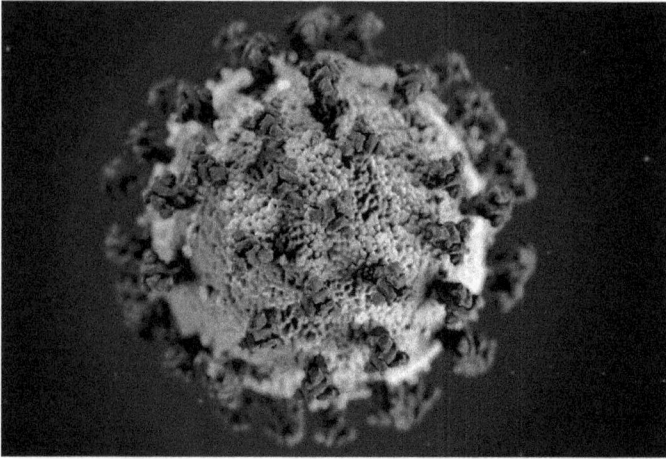

Fig. 1. CDC (Center For Disease Control) image of SARS-CoV-2.

Viral Narratives of Forgetting

The *New York Times Magazine's* "Decameron Project" presents an initial answer to this question. Published in early July 2020, the project asked twenty-nine contemporary authors to "write new short stories inspired by the moment." While most of the stories in the collection might be thought of as attempting to preserve the feelings and thoughts that swirled about at this chaotic cultural moment, Mona Awad's short story "A Blue Sky Like This" takes a different tack. Told from a second-person perspective, the story begins with a simple premise: "you" visit a shadowy clinic on your birthday to rid yourself of memories of 2020. After the fictional procedure, the newly unburdened protagonist wanders New York City like a modern-day Rip Van Winkle, marveling at the deserted shops, empty streets, and mask-clad taxi drivers before meeting up with her ex-husband, Ben, for what she thinks will be a friendly chat on a sunny afternoon at the park.

It isn't long before readers come to realize the limitations of the protagonist's pollyannaish worldview. Sitting on the far side of a bench he has just disinfected, Ben tells "you" he "fucked up the other night," and you strusggle to recall the circumstances, taking him to mean that the two of you had sex. After all, what other reason could there be to frame a physical encounter in this way? But the structure of Ben's responses implies that all he had done the other night was bring you your groceries after you told him you were sick. When he heard you sobbing, he opened the door to your apartment, breaking social distancing protocols to give you some relief from your months of isolation, while at the same time risking exposure to the deadly and never named SARS-CoV-2 virus.

By the time that Awad's story was published on July 8th, New York City's COVID-19 cases were three months removed from their devastating first peak in early April 2020. The story's ironic conceit — a protagonist willfully ignoring her transformed world — seems in part an attempt to represent the coping mechanisms of traumatized New Yorkers living in this period. At the same time, readers who reconstruct the plot are given a kind of memorial to the feelings (dread and loneliness), the body language (removed), and the objects (masks and hand wipes) of a crisis in the process of dissipating. We are asked to remember a moment when "fucking up" meant encountering another with a "bare, glowing face" rather than a mask. More generally, the story seems to frame the never-named virus from some future vantage point in which it has been forgotten, like the Spanish flu virus of 1918, which countless op-eds have also reminded us we worked hard to forget. And, in our imagined future neglect of the virus, we also neglect the lives of the people who have lived and died through its life.

This neglect can have devastating biological consequences because viruses need to be neglected or forgotten in order to take on the features of what we call life. Unlike every other known organism on our planet, viruses cycle back and forth between what approximates active life and dormant non-life depending on their environments. Viruses such as SARS-CoV-2 certainly resemble other life forms. After all, they contain complex biomolecules including DNA or RNA and certain protein structures that we associate with living creatures. However, because they lack complex cellular structures called organelles, they are incapable of producing and expending energy to perform certain fundamental tasks that we associate with other living beings. Most importantly, viruses cannot reproduce themselves, a fundamental characteristic of living things, which is why they are often excluded from philosophical discussions of life. Instead, they trick the complex systems of other living matter — bacteria, plants, animals, and so on — to perform that work for them.

Of course, the bodies of other organisms often resist performing such actions and have developed a dizzying set of strategies to prevent viral encounters or eradicate viral infections. In the case of humans, our immune responses are governed by our various white blood cells, which the body tasks with recognizing and eliminating either the virus itself or cells infected with the virus. If a virus is to foster "life" and continue to pass on copies of itself, it must adopt one of two strategies. On the one hand, an acute viral infection can overwhelm these agents of our immune system and eventually kill us, requiring the virus to find a new host. On the other, a chronic viral infection might evade detection by such cells and, sometimes, like the many other benign microorganisms within us, enter permanently into what scientists call our "metagenome," fusing its DNA harmlessly with our own. In both scenarios, a virus's capacity to live and to carry out the work of reproduction depends upon what might be called its biological charisma, that is, how it compels or does not compel our bodies to pay attention to it. When we neglect a virus, it succeeds.

A similar process operates on the social scale of human behavior. Here again, unlike so many organisms, viruses thrive when they are least charismatic to us. As one would imagine, a virus becomes charismatic when we perceive it as an immediate threat to our individual lives. When a virus produces acute infections, as was the case with SARS-CoV-2 in March 2020 in

New York City, the city and state introduced a set of biological, political, and social initiatives to stop it from creating more life. The success of such strategies, of course, relies upon the proper recognition of the virus — how it looks, how it behaves, how it spreads, and whom it affects — leading to the normalization of those masks and sheltering-in-place procedures that Awad's protagonist finds so puzzling after her procedure. However, the uneven social, demographic, and political landscapes of the United States mean that elsewhere in the country, the virus is perceived in the same manner that Awad's memory-cleansed protagonist perceives it: as a matter of no concern. Driven by a federal government unwilling to trace and contain the spread of SARS-CoV-2, the virus spread quickly in the days following Awad's publication, ravaging southern, western, and midwestern states and inflicting a disproportionate amount of suffering upon people of color.

As the second wave of COVID-19 in late July 2020 and the even larger Delta and Omicron waves in 2021 and 2022 have revealed, the neglected lives of other humans as well as the neglected lives of viruses depend upon our ability, or inability, to retain memories of the disease, not only the biological memories of T-cells within our body but, as Awad's protagonist suggests, the memory of recent behaviors, objects, and feelings that some people desperately wish to put behind themselves. This interdependency is implied at the end of Awad's story when the protagonist reaches her hand across the park bench to touch Ben. As he recoils from her and gets up to leave, "you" blissfully wave to him and to other socially distanced park-goers, who, the narrator notes, "gape at you in horror. Which is just so tragic. What is there to be afraid of on a day like this? Under a blue sky like this? Such a beautiful day?" What makes such a seemingly innocuous conclusion so horrifying is the protagonist herself and her steadfast determination to forget the virus. After recovering from, one suspects, a relatively minor case of COVID-19, "you" project your own experiences onto those around "you." "You" are oblivious to the thousands of New Yorkers who cannot simply return to pre-COVID normalcy because they have lost their lives, their livelihoods, and their loved ones.

Worse, in neglecting the quasi-life of the virus, the protagonist continues to put those human lives at risk, and in this respect, the story is depressingly prophetic. Less than four months after Awad's story was published, Donald Trump echoed the protagonist's sentiment in his sanguine response to his own COVID experiences. After receiving experimental treatment unavailable to the general public, Trump tweeted: "Feeling really good! Don't be afraid of Covid. Don't let it dominate your life." Within a month, new cases of the virus had doubled within the United States as viral fatigue grew. This third wave, like the second wave in the summer of 2020 and the later Delta and Omicron waves, provides a sharp justification for why we need to hold onto these painful memories of viral lives. As the horrified onlookers in Awad's story insist, to do otherwise is to abdicate our responsibilities to the most vulnerable members of our communities, those whom the narrative asks us to remember in Awad's brutally ironic ending.

Perhaps unintentionally, Awad's story might also be thought of as an ironic commentary on the decision by the *New York Times* to call the collection "The Decameron Project." The title alludes to Giovanni Boccaccio's famous work written in the wake of the Black Death in Europe during the fourteenth century. Ostensibly, the editors made this decision to enlist the bubonic plague to better understand the ongoing COVID-19 crisis, linking the viral outbreak of the present to a devastating bacteriological outbreak of the past. But Boccacio's time seemed to suffer from the same problem of retaining the memory of plague as our own. In the opening frame story, we are introduced to ten young men and women who, presumably ignoring local quarantines, travel from the bubonic-plague-infested city of Florence to the deserted countryside of Fiesole. Over their two-week stay, they entertain themselves with stories that often have little to do with the horrors they have just witnessed. Like Awad's protagonist, then, these storytellers also use fiction to neglect the lives of pathogens and people around them.

Tracing Viral Loads

This is not, of course, to say that the story of the virus in human history is simply the story of willful neglect. While viruses have been a continuous presence in the natural history of human beings, until the last half century, they did not appear (as themselves) in our social histories for two seemingly antithetical reasons. Though each individual virus is incredibly small, the effects of viruses in aggregate can stretch to enormous mathematical scales. As such, these microorganisms make extraordinary demands upon our imaginations. They ask us to see not only these strange quasi-creatures but also *ourselves* from the perspective of the population rather than that of the individual.

A typical virus is about 1/10,000th of a millimeter in diameter, making it invisible both to the human eye and to the light microscopes developed in Europe in the seventeenth and eighteenth century. Given this invisibility, for the bulk of human history, viruses were purely speculative concepts and were often treated as inanimate poisons rather than rapidly replicating biological agents. In classical Latin, for example, "virus" means "snake venom," and this sense of the term persisted in Europe until the early twentieth century. The association of virus and venom can be traced to classical stories of the rabies virus, most notably in the Greek and Roman myth of Kerberos, the beastly dog of the underworld whose saliva is associated with the venom of snakes.

While obviously inaccurate, this model made sense for the rabies virus because, like poisons, rabies affects only the person who receives the fatal dog or bat bite. Most other viruses, however, can be transmitted from human to human after they are replicated in their host, something no poison can do. As we now know, viruses become recognizable diseases when their "load," or the number of viral copies in our bodies, reaches a certain threshold. For SARS-CoV-2, current research suggests that that load is unfathomably large, ranging from around 25,000 copies per mL of sputum to around 600 copies per mL of blood. The viral tendency towards exponential growth made it possible for humans to see a virus. By the end of the nineteenth century, advances in light-microscope technology enabled scientists to make out blurry viral clusters on slides, but it was not until the 1930s that electron microscopes led to a more complete understanding of a single virus's complex protein and nucleic acid structures. As such, while viruses have been with us for hundreds of thousands of years, they have been fully present to us for only about fifty years and even then, only in aggregate.

We rely upon a similar principle of aggregation when we try to make viruses visible across geographical scales. Because they replicate so quickly, contagious viruses are easily transmitted through the myriad, invisible social networks that surround us. As Priscilla Wald argues, these networks are temporarily thrown into relief during viral outbreaks, where "the circulation of microbes materializes the transmission of ideas. The interactions that make us sick also constitute us as a community" (Wald 2008, 2). But in order for us to imagine that "community" in any comprehensible way, this narrative of contract tracing, like the viral clusters on a slide, needs to be localized to small geographical spaces.

Early narratives of disease tend to view them through this metaphorical lens, framing local outbreaks as divine punishment for individual transgressions within a local community. At the beginning of Homer's *Iliad,* for example, the disease that ravages the Greek soldiers is brought by Apollo as punishment for the Greek general Agamemnon's decision to take the daughter of his priest as a slave. Likewise, Sophocles' *Oedipus Rex* begins with a devastating plague brought to Thebes by the king's fatal lack of self-knowledge:

> A blight is on the fruitful plants of the earth,
> a blight is on the cattle in the fields,
> a blight is on our women that no children
> are born to them; a God that carries fire,
> a deadly pestilence, is on our town,
> strikes us and spares not, and the house of Cadmus

is emptied of its people while black Death
grows rich in groaning and in lamentation. (2010, 12)

As human populations have become more mobile, the processes
of contact tracing and, by extension, our ability to tell comprehensible stories about viruses within communities become
more challenging. Since the 1970s and 1980s, biochemists and
public health officials have developed increasingly sophisticated
models for viral replication and transmission. But this theoreti-
cal knowledge does not mean that we have even partially mas-
tered the multiplying lives of viruses as they exist in our immediate realities. Since the spring of 2020, for example, American
public health workers have frantically attempted to trace how
SARS-CoV-2 moves between human communities. As cases rose
in the fall, however, these efforts were abandoned in many states
as accidental transmissions of the virus swept across networks
of dizzying complexity. How, then, might we imagine the life of
a virus that replicates hundreds of thousands of times within us
and that has brought into the same network street vendors in
Wuhan, balcony singers in Naples, and motorcycle enthusiasts
in South Dakota? And, as the virus has begun to mutate in light
of this rapid replication, bringing new UK, Brazilian, and South
African variants into the world, which variations in our own
worldview will emerge?

Clearly, we need to rethink our sense of scale if we are to begin telling more compelling stories about the viruses that help to
shape our identities as individuals and as a population. Some of
this work has already been done. Because of their ability to in-
voke complex networks, viral pathways have inspired new ways
of thinking about human social and technological networks in
the fields of information science. Most notably, the fact that, unlike bacteria, viruses actively harness the biological systems of
their host to replicate proved an irresistible metaphor for Richard Dawkins, who coined the term "meme" in his 1976 monograph *The Selfish Gene* to describe ideas or behaviors that "go viral," reproducing themselves across human networks. The same
reproductive structure led the computer scientist Fred Cohen,

in his PhD thesis, to coin the phrase "computer virus," which he defined as "a program that can infect other programs by modifying them to include a, possibly evolved, version of itself" (1986, 10). Like biological viruses, these memes and computer viruses respond to the various selective pressures of our emerging globalized society, changing to suit their ever-changing political, economic and social environments.

Drawing upon these analogies, literary artists are beginning to consider the ways in which viral networks can help us tell new stories about the lives of human populations. A second story from *The New York Times* "Decameron Project," Charles Yu's "Systems" (2020), offers a fascinating glimpse into this new direction of storytelling. The characters and plot of Yu's story look nothing like those in a conventional narrative. In place of the vibrant, ironic voice of Awad's narrator, "Systems" is delivered in spare prose by the collective consciousness of the virus itself. As it tries to tell the story of the American population during the COVID-19 crisis, this aggregate narrator faces the same challenges as the late nineteenth-century scientists who could only view viruses in clusters. To minimize human complexity, the narrators flatten our differences into a set of algorithmic behaviors within a larger system. In late 2019, as the story begins, American behavior is represented by a series of web searches that reduce individual behavior into a series of Dawkinsian memes.

They search for things:

Harry and meghan
hary and megan Canada
new year's resolution
new year's resolutions how long

They like being with their families. They like being with strangers. They work in small spaces. Crowd into boxes, push the air around. Sleep in boxes. Need each other. Touch each other. They move around the world. Everywhere in the world. Like us.

Aside from the idiosyncratic, comic misspellings of Prince Harry's and Meghan Markle's names (at the time, the couple was in the midst of relocating to Canada after relinquishing their royal duties), the viral narrator privileges pattern over difference, viewing its hosts' actions through its own peculiar perspective, what the biologist Jakob von Uexküll would call its *Umwelt*, or lived reality. By seeing the world through the alien *Umwelt* of the virus, Yu defamiliarizes both the setting of human drama (houses, stores, and airports) and the human actions that are typically at the forefront of human narrative. In the process, the viral narrators find a surprising kinship with their hosts: "They harness invisible forces. Electromagnetism. Light. They are like us. They have codes. Codes of symbolic sequences. They encode information and spread it."

Yu's narrative may seem to efface political responsibility in its emphasis on nameless "systems" rather than individuals. At the same time, the story's preoccupation with those same "systems" creates an allegorical structure for collective action that Awad's protagonist, focused on the lives of individual humans, cannot. In its most successful moments, Yu's narrative knits together the viral and social histories of 2020, showing how the virus's devastating impact on minority communities dovetails with the coeval, collectivist Black Lives Matter movement galvanized by the killings of Eric Garner, Breonna Taylor, and George Floyd. Knitting together both anti-police violence protests and anti-mask protests, the narrator coolly observes: "Some of them enjoy breathing as their right. / Some of them can't breathe." Through this allusion to Eric Garner's and George Floyd's final words, Yu asks his readers to consider not only the relationship between right-wing public health attitudes and racialized violence but also the more complicated calculus of how or whether to gather together to protest that violence under pandemic conditions. This calculus provoked changes in American search terms, where "they search for things: / where is protest / safe to protest / how to protest / They realize: / Community is how it spreads. / Community is how it is solved." Echoing Wald's and Dawkins's observations about the movement of ideas, Yu asks us to consider the transmission of SARS-CoV-2 alongside the virulent transmission of racist ideology, calling upon us to change the way that we interact with and envision community.

As Yu's story reveals, attending to the lives of viruses can help us to rethink our notion of human community at a critical moment for our species. Alongside the "viral load" thresholds that make us sick, we might begin to consider how our ideas and actions — our tweets and our masking protocols — are less individual behaviors and more aggregate loads that influence our world for better or for worse. In the months since the story was published, these loads have brought more of both into view. Fanned by conspiratorial rhetoric regarding the "Chinese flu" on social media, anti-Asian violence has increased in the United States, culminating in a deadly mass shooting at three spas in Atlanta, Georgia. At the same time, new online and in-person community organizations have emerged to combat this toxic ideology and to support vulnerable peoples of color left behind by the failed national responses to the pandemic, including, for instance, the Mutual Aid Hub and the Black Lives Matter Survival Fund. Learning how to imagine and manage these conflicting loads as we also manage the viral outbreak will be crucial for the long-term health of our population and our planet.

References and Further Reading

Awad, Mona. 2020. "A Blue Sky Like This." *The New York Times,* July 7. https://www.nytimes.com/interactive/2020/07/07/magazine/awad-blue-short-story.html.

"Introducing the Black Lives Matter Survival Fund." n.d. *Black Lives Matter.* https://blacklivesmatter.com/survival-fund/.

Boccaccio, Giovanni. 2003. *The Decameron.* Translated by G.H. McWilliam. New York: Penguin Classics.

Cohen, Fred. 1986. "Computer Viruses." Phd Thesis, Unversity of Southern California, Los Angeles.

Dawkins, Richard. 1976. *The Selfish Gene.* Oxford: Oxford University Press.

Homer. 2007. *The Iliad.* Translated by Rodney Merrill. Ann Arbor: University of Michigan Press.

Sophocles. 2010. *Oedipus The King.* Translated by David Grene. Chicago: University of Chicago Press.

von Uexküll, Jakob. 2010. *A Foray into the World of Animals and Humans, with a Theory of Meaning.* Translated by Joseph D. O'Neil. Minneapolis: University of Minnesota Press.

Wald, Priscilla. 2008. *Contagious: Cultures, Carriers, and the Outbreak Narrative.* Durham: Duke University Press.

Yu, Charles. 2020. "Systems." *The New York Times,* July 7. https://www.nytimes.com/interactive/2020/07/07/magazine/charles-yu-short-story.html.

Contributor Biographies

Karen Leona Anderson is Associate Professor of English at St. Mary's College of Maryland. She is the author of two collections of poetry, *Punish honey* (Carolina Wren) and *Receipt* (Milkweed Editions). Her scholarly and creative work has appeared in numerous journals and anthologies including the ecolanguage reader, *The Ecopoetry Anthology,* and *The Best American Poetry.* Her most recent scholarly work is on Emily Dickinson, fungi, and scale shifting.

As the granddaughter of two German foresters, **Helga G. Braunbeck** grew up close to nature. Her first garden was a mini-forest of small trees transplanted from the real forest. She moved on to study German and English literature in Tübingen/ Germany, Oregon, and California and is now Professor of German Studies at North Carolina State University in Raleigh, NC. Her two books discuss issues of authorship in East-German writer Christa Wolf, and intermediality in the work of Prague German author Libuše Moníková. After her second book, she turned her attention to the environmental humanities and became especially interested in literary and cultural plant studies. She has published about Klaus Modick's novella *Moss,* lignite mining in German culture, and the impact of the Anthropocene on gardens and gardening in recent German literature. Her current projects focus on plant poetics and literary representations of arboreal imaginaries. And her current garden is filled with flowers, veggies, wildlife, and more than sixty trees. The older ones are covered in lovely moss and lichen.

Damien Bright is a Research Associate at the Institute for Advanced Sustainability Studies in Potsdam, Germany. He received his PhD in Anthropology from the University of Chicago in 2022. Damien's research engages critical natural history, animal studies, and the psychosocial dimensions of modernist technoscience. He is currently conducting a multi-sited ethnographic investigation of the technopolitical dimensions of ocean engineering as part of the EU-funded OceanNETs consortium. *Whither the Reef?*, his first book manuscript, is in preparation and builds on his dissertation research into efforts to salvage the Great Barrier Reef from its predicted demise. The book explains the practical and moral quandaries that the sciences of marine life encounter, along with their supporters and detractors, in the push to design large-scale and largely experimental "interventions" in the name of planetary care. Damien's writing has appeared in Techniques & Culture and Diseña.

Joela Jacobs is Assistant Professor of German Studies at the University of Arizona and founder of the Literary and Cultural Plant Studies Network (plants.arizona.edu). Her research focuses on nineteenth- to twenty-first-century German literature and its intersections with the environmental humanities, specifically plants, animals, and environmentalist culture, as well as Jewish studies, the history of sexuality, and the history of science. She has published on monstrosity, multilingualism, literary censorship, biopolitics, animal epistemology, zoopoetics, phytopoetics, cultural environmentalism, and contemporary German Jewish identity.

Dani Lamorte is a Pittsburgh-based artist working in performance, video, photography, and text. He has performed and shown work at the Andy Warhol Museum (Pittsburgh), University of Arizona Museum of Art (Tucson), Human Resources (Los Angeles), Whippersnapper Gallery (Toronto), Studio Beluga (Montréal), and Mattress Factory (Pittsburgh). Dani is a contributing writer for *Cleveland Review of Books* and has published essays in *Edge Effects, Sundog Lit,* and *Journal of Critical Library & Information Studies.* Dani's first book of essays, *Of Fakes,* is under contract with the University Press of Kentucky.

Raymond Malewitz is Associate Professor of English at Oregon State University. He is the author of one monograph, *The Practice of Misuse* (Stanford University Press, 2014), and is at work on a second, tentatively entitled "Epizootic Encounters: A Cultural History of Animal Disease." His work has appeared in journals such as *Critical Inquiry, PMLA, Modern Fiction Studies,* and *Configurations* as well as more popular venues such as *The Washington Post.*

Agnes Malinowska is Assistant Instructional Professor in the MA Program in the Humanities and in English at the University of Chicago. Her teaching and research focuses on American modernism and modernity, nonhuman studies, the history of science, and gender and sexuality studies. Agnes's recent writing appears in the journal *Modernism/modernity.*

Ada Smailbegović is Assistant Professor of English at Brown University. She is the author of *Poetics of Liveliness: Molecules, Fibers, Tissues, Clouds* (Columbia, 2021) and a cofounder of the digital publishing platform the Organism for Poetic Research. Her published essays and poetic work have appeared in a variety of venues, including *differences, Comparative Literature, Triple Canopy,* and *angelaki.*

www.ingramcontent.com/pod-product-compliance
Lightning Source LLC
Chambersburg PA
CBHW050654270326
41927CB00012B/3024